Collaborative Creativity

Also by Robert Kelly

CREATIVE DEVELOPMENT: TRANSFORMING EDUCATION THROUGH DESIGN THINKING, INNOVATION, AND INVENTION **(2016)**

EDUCATING FOR CREATIVITY: A GLOBAL CONVERSATION **(2012)**

CREATIVE EXPRESSION, CREATIVE EDUCATION: CREATIVITY AS A PRIMARY RATIONALE FOR EDUCATION **(COEDITED WITH CARL LEGGO, 2008)**

Collaborative Creativity

Educating for Creative Development, Innovation, and Entrepreneurship

ROBERT KELLY

Brush
Education Inc.

20 21 22 23 24 5 4 3 2 1

Printed and manufactured in Canada

Brush Education Inc.

www.brusheducation.ca

contact@brusheducation.ca

Cover and interior design: Carol Dragich, Dragich Design

Cover images: istockphoto.com/hakkiarslan; istockphoto.com/Hesti Pranowo

Library and Archives Canada Cataloguing in Publication

Title: Collaborative creativity : educating for creative development, innovation, and entrepreneurship / Robert Kelly.

Names: Kelly, Robert W., author.

Description: Includes bibliographical references and index.

Identifiers: Canadiana (print) 20190232455 | Canadiana (ebook) 20190232730 | ISBN 9781550598377 (softcover) | ISBN 9781550598384 (PDF) | ISBN 9781550598391 (Kindle) | ISBN 9781550598407 (EPUB)

Subjects: LCSH: Creative ability—Study and teaching. | LCSH: Creative teaching.

Classification: LCC LB1062 .K452020 | DDC 370.15/7—dc23

We acknowledge the support of the Government of Canada
Nous reconnaissons l'appui du gouvernement du Canada | Canadä

Dedication

This volume is dedicated
to our daughter Katie,
whose unconditional love and acceptance
of everyone and everything
is an inspiration to all.

Contents

Acknowledgements

I would like to thank all of the professional contributors to this book, who gave freely of their time and expertise despite busy schedules to create the Collaborating to Create features in this volume.

I would like to thank the professional educators who are also graduate students in the Collaborative Creativity & Design Thinking for Innovation graduate program in the Werklund School of Education at the University of Calgary for their contributions to this volume and their profound dedication to collaborative creativity and innovation for the benefit of others in their professional environments.

I would like to thank Stephanie Bartlett, Erin Quinn, and Carla-Jayne Samuelson for contributing their collective expertise and design acumen to the ongoing design, delivery, and relentless prototyping of the Collaborative Creativity & Design Thinking for Innovation graduate program.

INTRODUCTION

Collaboration + Creativity

A MATCH MADE IN HEAVEN, DESPERATELY NEEDED ON EARTH

Recently, I was driving home from the University of Calgary on a beautiful summer evening, heading about a half hour west of the city to where I live in the shadow of the Rocky Mountains. The sun was just beginning to set. There were only a few clouds on the horizon. I had a 180-degree view of this incredible panorama of mountain and sky. I never tire of this drive. I was driving my late model Subaru Crosstrek (and no, this is not an advertisement for the Japanese Subaru corporation). It is orange. I chose orange because I thought of it as a passive safety feature making my vehicle more visible. One thing is for sure: I have very little trouble finding my car in a large parking lot. I didn't purchase this vehicle, however, because of any potential passive safety feature. I purchased it for the active safety features. My car is semiautonomous. It is loaded with safety features that operate on their own without me having to initiate them. One of these features is lane-keep-assist. If you begin to drift or sway, and cross into another lane without signalling, you get a visual and audible alert, and the car will even intervene and steer you back into your lane. It detects side-to-side sway if you're falling asleep while driving. It is very unnerving to experience something else steering your car for the first time. It takes a while to learn to trust the technology. When you think of it, we trust technology every day, so why should this be different?

On this particular evening, the traffic was very light as I drove home in the right-hand westward lane of a four-lane highway. I thought it would be a good time to try a simple experiment with this technology as a way to help me trust the technology more. (Please do not try this at home.) I waited until the road was banked a little to the left and then took my hands off the steering wheel. The car drifted to the left, and was just about to cross the dotted line between the two westbound lanes, when lane-keep-assist kicked in and steered my car back into the middle of the right lane. Next, I took my hands off the steering wheel again, when the car was banking to the right. Just as the car was about to cross the solid white line that marked the outside boundary of the right lane, not only did the lane-keep-assist steer me back to the middle of the lane, but it gave me an audio warning and a visual warning that came up on the screen: "Put your hands on the steering wheel." I was busted by my car. *It* didn't trust *me*.

In 2016, Håkan Samuelsson, the CEO of Volvo, proclaimed "no one will die in a new Volvo car in four years." Volvo had identified speeding, intoxication, and distraction as the primary factors in vehicle-related deaths and major injuries. Its aim was to tackle these factors to work toward a zero-accident goal. By the time you are reading this passage, we will have started to learn whether Volvo was successful in reaching this goal. For obvious reasons, there will be situations where people die in vehicles despite advanced technology, but there is no doubt that the probability of accidents has gone down, and will continue to go down dramatically, with advancing safety features. Technology is advancing rapidly to the point where manufacturers are planning fully autonomous electric fleets and beyond, no doubt to include individual autonomous flying vehicles. Corporations have been prototyping these for years. French inventor Franky Zapata has flown over the English Channel in 22 minutes on a hoverboard. In 1985, Marty McFly's hoverboard in the first *Back to the Future* movie was Hollywood fiction. Will the internal combustion engine automobile become obsolete? It is only a matter of time. Rapid change is happening across sociocultural, economic, technological, and environmental sectors, and the rate of change is getting faster.

As change marches on and surrounds us, we adapt bit by bit in response to identifiable trends that are informed by research and statistics. If we look at the development of the internal combustion vehicle over the last several decades, we can see profound changes and innovations to improve safety standards and fuel efficiency. My orange vehicle is an example of this. In education, too, there have been innumerable attempts to bring innovation to mainstream educational practice, as educators work hard to think outside the box and innovate to adapt to change. Inquiry-based learning, project-based learning, personalized learning, and experiential learning are only some of the many examples of initiatives that any experienced educator will recognize in some form or other. However, as change progresses with increasing rapidity, existing models or ways of being in the world become obsolete, and adapting them becomes futile and irrelevant. Thinking outside the box implies that one is in a box, and that anything new or novel is relative to that box. The predominant educational model is a machine bureaucracy organizational structure that exists for standardization, largely through transferring curricular content and assessing its retention as a measure of educational success. This model is obsolete. Waks (2014) contends that "we will have to build new models of living in today's global network society, complete with new means of earning our livelihoods and new forms of learning aligned with them" (p. xi). He also maintains that retrofitting educational innovation onto the existing standardized, industrial-era, educational organizational structure results in the loss of the transformative potential of innovation, because of the inertia of the negative attributes of the box. He adds that against the backdrop of massive change, "it is a human invention that has outlived its utility" (p. xi).

In the following chapters, I will describe a completely different educational ecosystem that has the concepts of collaborative creativity and creative development at its core. This has become an educational imperative to meet a world that has changed dramatically. Emerging problems and their potential resolutions are complex. In 2016, the United Nations 17 Sustainable Development Goals were adopted by world leaders. The Sustainable Development Goals are the blueprint to achieve a better and more sustainable future for all. They address the global challenges we face, including poverty, inequality, climate, environmental degradation, prosperity, and peace and justice (United Nations, 2019). The Organisation of Economic Co-operation and Development (2018) complements these sustainable development goals by putting forward the following as part of its "Future of Education and Skills: Education 2030" initiative:

> New sources of growth are urgently needed to achieve stronger, more inclusive and more sustainable development. Innovation can offer vital solutions, at affordable cost, to economic, social and cultural dilemmas. Innovative economies are more productive, more resilient, more adaptable and better able to support higher living standards.
>
> To prepare for 2030, people should be able to think creatively, develop new products and services, new jobs, new processes and methods, new ways of thinking and living, new enterprises, new sectors, new business models and new social models. Increasingly, innovation springs not from individuals thinking and working alone,

> but through cooperation and collaboration with others to draw on existing knowledge to create new knowledge. The constructs that underpin the competency include adaptability, creativity, curiosity and open-mindedness. (p. 5)

The complex social, economic, and cultural challenges that lie before us require that creativity be a collaborative pursuit leveraging diversity and interconnectedness to maximize positive outcomes. They require more than creative individuals acting on their own. They require a view forward to bring interconnected, varied, and (frequently) distributed potential collaborators together to innovate for the benefit of others. This book presents the educational ecosystem of creative development through collaborative creativity as the way forward. This ecosystem requires the invention of a new educational space, not an adaptation of a counterproductive, obsolete educational box. As computer scientist Alan Kay once said, the best way to predict the future is to invent it.

This book speaks to educators, administrators, educational designers, government officials, and parents about a new way of being educationally in the world. It aims to inform the invention of new educational ecosystems that speak to collaborative creativity. It provides a view of what an educational culture of collaborative creativity could look like through a journey from Chapters 1 to 5 that goes from theory to practice.

Chapter 1, "The Concepts of Creativity, Collaboration, and Collaborative Creativity," establishes a clear, shared understanding of the concepts of creativity and collaboration, and the resultant combination of collaborative creativity, to enable application of these concepts in educational practice. Clarifying the general contexts for how each term is used, while differentiating these core words from related words and concepts, enables precision in the practical application of these concepts. This provides a foundational layer for this book.

Chapter 2, "The Transformative Dynamics of a New Educational Ecosystem," adds another foundational layer by describing in detail the transformational dynamics at play in the educational imperative to design and build educational ecosystems around the concept of collaborative creativity. These transformative dynamics revolve around certain primary dynamics: consume to create, passive to interactive, and authoritative to empowering. The consume-to-create dynamic is seen as central as we move from consumptive-intense educational practice to a highly interactive creativity-intense culture. These core dynamics are augmented by subdynamics: ego-centric to eco-centric, machine bureaucracy to adhocracy, competitive to collaborative, assets to access, didactic to dialogic, one-way to reciprocal, outcomes known to outcomes unknown, extrinsic motivation to intrinsic motivation, top-down to emergent design, measurement to development, and pedagogy to sociogogy. The core dynamics and subdynamics collectively inform the attributes of an educational culture of collaborative creativity.

Chapter 3, "A Framework for Collaborative Creativity in Educational Practice," begins by examining what has informed our beliefs about what education is. This includes reflecting on our own educational journeys and comparing them to longitudinal observations from the field, ranging from about early-childhood education to graduate-level postsecondary education. Chapter 3 then goes on to describe a creative-development ecosystem made up of nine interrelated developmental strands. It differentiates the collaborative creativity educational ecosystem from traditional educational discourses. Collaborative and communicative development are combined as developmental strands, and are foundational in amplifying the other interrelated developmental strands that make up the creative development framework. This chapter further examines considerations for learning-experience design and assessment design for an educational culture of collaborative creativity by discussing a design framework that progressively leads to learner-initiated invention and innovation.

Chapter 4, "Considerations for Establishing a Culture of Collaborative Creativity," focuses on establishing what the attributes of a collaborative culture look like through an exploration of the characteristics of shared vision, leveraged diversity, rotating leadership, meaningful communication, and the establishment of trust. This is accompanied by an exploration of factors that might preclude transitioning into an educational culture of collaborative creativity through the lens of our ingrained socialization in existing systems. This provides a baseline of observable components of collaborative culture that we can apply in the educational lab in Chapter 5 with graduate-level education students.

Chapter 5, "Giant Lobsters, Whales, and Elephants: A Case Study in Developing an Educational Culture of Collaborative Creativity," brings us right into the lab of teacher education. We take a journey with graduate students in education through a portion of a graduate program in education that I designed, and that I coordinate and teach at my home institution. The program is entitled Collaborative Creativity & Design Thinking for Innovation. We begin by examining design considerations for a teacher education program, whose specific aim is to establish a collaborative culture for educators to enable the design, development, and creation of original work in a wide range of creative contexts from social innovation to personal creative development. The chapter then takes the form of a metalogue where we hear the voices of the students and instructors through their reflections as they engage in an activity of collaborative creativity designed to establish a collaborative culture for the duration of the program. The metalogue covers the first part of the program, during a course entitled The Collaborative Culture of Creativity where 22 students, all professional educators from diverse educational backgrounds, are given the task of designing and building something as a group that none of them has designed or built before, and that would be next to impossible to design and build as an individual. The task is to build a giant lobster, approximately 9 metres (30 feet) long, that is anatomically correct, with correct proportions and no flat surfaces, made only of cardboard, paper, string, and duct tape. Previous program cohorts have built life-size humpback whales, orca whales, and African elephants. The metalogue provides valuable insights into the nuts and bolts of establishing an educational culture of collaborative creativity: it puts you in the front seat with educators who are experiencing, day by day, a transition into this culture.

Between chapters, features entitled Collaborating to Create present experts, from a variety of international and cultural educational contexts, talking about their diverse perspectives on the concept of an educational culture of collaborative creativity.

This book is an invitation to explore and question what we have come to know about education, and to give permission to invent and design a new way of being educationally in the world that is relevant to educators and learners in a time marked by rapid sociocultural, economic, technological, and environmental change. It is an invitation to develop an entrepreneurial disposition to imagine new ways to solve problems and create value, where entrepreneurship embraces initiatives that exist for the benefit of others and not just traditional profit taking. It is an invitation to embark on a new educational journey that empowers educators and learners through collaborative creativity. It is an invitation to live and embody collaborative creativity as educators. Enjoy the ride.

1

The Concepts of Creativity, Collaboration, and Collaborative Creativity

A clear, shared understanding of the concepts of creativity and collaboration, and the combined concept of collaborative creativity, must be established before we can apply these concepts in educational practice. Clarifying the general contexts for using these terms in this book, and differentiating these core words from related words and concepts, enables precision in the practical application of these concepts. All of these terms are subject to diverse interpretations in conversational and practical use and application. The general usage of these terms often lacks differentiation from associated terms (Gotz, 1981).

In general usage, the word *creativity* is often used interchangeably with the concepts of originality, innovation, divergent thinking, and idea generation. Each of these concepts, however, though closely associated with the word *creativity* and the concept of creative process, is distinctly different from the others.

The word *collaboration* is often used interchangeably with the word *cooperation* and even sometimes appears as a proxy for a sort of mass compliance among members of a group or organization with an organization initiative. As with the word *creativity*, the word *collaboration* is often used in diverse contexts as a substitute for associated words.

Collaborative creativity, the central focus of this book, and its foundational concepts of creativity and collaboration, are viewed through the lenses of applications within educational practice. Educational practice encompasses facilitation of the application of collaborative creativity to educator training, macro curricular and pedagogical design, learning experience and assessment design, and the design of supportive physical and virtual environments that are conducive to an educational culture of collaborative creativity.

The Concept of Creativity

The Definition and Vocabulary of Creativity

The etymology of the word *creativity* is rooted in the Latin word *creare* meaning to make or produce in a physical sense (Gotz, 1981; Piirto, 2004). The implication here is that the activity has observable physical results. Piirto adds that "to be 'creative' is to be 'originative.' *Originative* implies to make something new. *To be creative, then, is to make something new or novel*" (p. 6). There is an implied process here, that creativity involves moving from thought to form. Sawyer (2012) adds:

> Creativity researchers can't study what they can't see. This is why the scientific definition of creativity must exclude ideas that stay in a person's head and are never expressed, and ideas that no one else can see or understand. Under this definition your nightly dreams are not creative; ideas you have but never write down or communicate to anyone else aren't creative. (p. 7)

Lubart's (2000) definition of creativity as "a sequence of thoughts and actions that leads to novel adaptive production" (p. 295) is a foundational definition of the concept of creativity that reflects the core definitional attributes of the word *creativity*. It is important to keep in mind the three attributes of this definition: it will clarify usage and application in an educational context and preclude confusion with other related terms. The three identifiable attributes include:

- **a sequence of thoughts:** imagination and ideation that lead to actions
- **a sequence of actions:** the making of an observable physical form in the currency of the discipline or field where the creative production occurs
- **novel, adaptive production:** a creative, physical outcome that displays original or novel qualities

It is important to note that these three components are interwoven and don't necessarily occur in a linear fashion. They are useful in differentiating and contextualizing related vocabulary when discussing and applying the terms *creativity* and *creative process* in educational practice.

Wallas (1926), in his work *Art of Thought*, presented one of the first models of the creative process. The Wallas stage model has four steps:

- **preparation:** preparatory work on a problem that focuses the individual's mind on the problem and explores the problem's dimensions

- **incubation:** where the problem is internalized into the subconscious mind and nothing appears externally to be happening
- **illumination or insight:** where the creative idea bursts forth from its subconscious processing into conscious awareness
- **verification:** where the idea is consciously verified, elaborated, and then applied

The Wallas stage model of the creative process embodies the foundational tenets of moving from thought to tangible form. This early stage model informed many variations of creative-process stage theory in the decades that followed. During that time, a general transition occurred in the perception of the creative process: from the idea that the creative process largely exists in the realm of the subconscious to the idea that it can be deliberately enhanced through actions such as ideation, as Osborn (1963) elaborated.

American psychologist J. P. Guilford's (1959) benchmark work regarding traits of creative individuals expanded the vocabulary in this field with many terms closely associated with the concept of creativity. His traits of creative individuals encompass the following:

- **fluency of thinking:** the ability to think effortlessly, especially in ideation
- **flexibility in thinking:** the capacity to readily abandon old ideas and accept new ones
- **originality:** the capacity to come up with unusual ideas that are remote from previous concepts
- **redefinition:** the capacity to give up old interpretations of concepts or objects, and replace them with new ones
- **elaboration:** the capacity to fill in details or to add details to a general scheme
- **tolerance of ambiguity:** the willingness to accept some uncertainty, precluding rigidity in thinking
- **convergent thinking:** thinking toward a solution or problem resolution by sorting through possible alternatives
- **divergent thinking:** open-ended thinking and the generation of numerous potential problem-resolution alternatives

All of these terms are closely related to the concept of creativity, but are not synonymous with the concept of creativity. The terms *divergent thinking* and *originality* are often used interchangeably with the word *creativity*, yet they refer to a specific component of creative process or characteristic of creative process. They are not wholly substitutes for the word *creativity*. *Divergent thinking* refers to the generation of alternatives that are potential problem resolutions. Divergent thinking is part of the longitudinal thought-to-form process, albeit an important part, but it is not the complete process. *Originality* refers to an attribute of a creative outcome. Starko (2010) describes formal assessments of creativity, such as the Torrance Test for Creative Thinking, as tests, fundamentally, of divergent thinking capacity. Kaufmann, Plucker, and Baer (2008) comment on how the history of creativity assessment has focused on the assessment of divergent thinking capacity. They remark that, ironically, there has been little divergence in the field of testing creativity. A test of divergent thinking is not a test of creativity. It is a test of a component of creative process and may be an indicator of creative potential, but it is not a test of creativity.

Plucker, Beghetto, and Dow (2004) echo the core attributes of Lubart's (2000) definition and add the importance of the social context of the production's utility and novelty: "the interaction among aptitude, process, and environment by which an individual or group produces a perceptible product that is both novel and useful as defined within a social context" (p. 90). The addition of social context speaks to how a production, when one has engaged in a sequence of thoughts and actions, is perceived as creative or not. To examine this further, one has to keep in mind that the focus of this book is the application of these concepts in educational practice from early childhood to higher education, and that these concepts would apply to a learner at various stages of development—stages of development that span the abilities of a preschool-age child and an adult engaged in postsecondary graduate studies. Creative development is defined as the growth in creative capacity of an individual or group over time (Kelly, 2016). Creative capacity is defined as the level of complexity an individual or group can command to engage in creative practice at a point in time (Kelly, 2016).

Definitional Contexts for Assessing Creative Outcomes

Sawyer (2012) describes two definitional contexts for the concept of creativity that lend themselves to educational application: individualistic and sociocultural. These two definitional contexts revolve around the context in which the originality of a production is assessed. Guilford (1959) defines originality as a response that is unusual, atypical, or remote. Simonton (2016) describes original ideas and outcomes as having low initial probability, compared to ideas and outcomes that are less original or are unoriginal, which have a high initial probability with greater frequency and predictability. In an educational context, the question arises as to how to assess the degree of originality of the problem resolution of a learner. What should be compared to the learner's outcome, to assess its remoteness and probability and ultimately its degree of originality? Sawyer's (2012) dual contexts perhaps point the way. Sawyer defines creativity in the individualistic context as "a new mental combination that is expressed in the world" (p. 7). The originality of work produced in this context is compared to the previous work of that particular individual, whether or not that particular outcome has been produced elsewhere by another individual or in another social context. He defines creativity in the sociocultural context as "the generation of a product that is judged to be novel and also to be appropriate, useful or valuable by a suitably knowledgeable social group" (p. 8). The degree of originality of the creative outcome is assessed by members of a social group from the field or domain where the creative outcome took place.

For example, if an educator were to track the creative writing of an 8-year-old student in their elementary classroom over the course of the school year, the educator would be able to discern whether the learner made some leaps in originality developmentally through longitudinal observation and familiarity from daily interaction with the student. This would embody the application of Sawyer's (2012) individualistic lens. Any low probability or remote developments, compared to previous production, would come to the fore in a variety of ways spanning character development, plot development and sophistication, and the use of vocabulary and metaphor. These are all observable phenomena to a well-trained educator working on a daily basis with a student toward growth in the learner's creative capacity and development. To apply Sawyer's (2012) sociocultural lens to this educational context would not be conducive to creative development. The sociocultural lens is typically applied to those functioning at the top of their field or domain. Those established in academia, business and industry, and the arts are typically assessed through this lens of creativity and originality by peers within those fields and domains. In Kelly (2016), I explain that "it is educationally inappropriate and unrealistic to compare creative production from a young learner to creative practitioners at the top of their respective fields to assess whether the learner's response is original or not" (p. 3). I elaborate further:

> When facilitating creative development, it is more useful and productive to assess a learner's response for its degree of originality relative to the past creative production outcomes of the learner

> (Starko, 2010). This creates developmental space for reachable, realistic goals for creative development over time without the onerous constant comparisons to mature, creative producers who have developed work through intense research and experimentation over considerable periods of time or even lifetimes. (p. 3)

This doesn't preclude using accomplished creative practitioners as inspiration, research resources, or as aspirational goals. Sawyer's (2012) individualistic and sociocultural definitional lenses are both relevant to the educational journey of an individual from early childhood to higher education. In Kelly (2016), I further elaborate on the appropriate blending of these definitional lenses in educational application over time, starting with the individualistic lens in a learner's formative years and gradually evolving to the sociocultural lens as the learner's work grows in complexity and gains relevance to the field or domain where it takes place:

> In an educational context, it is important to apply a sliding or evolving definition to the concepts of creativity and originality in education to enable the operationalization of systematic and continuous creative development over a learner's educational and life journey. This respects the diverse developmental paces in creative growth of individual learners by assessing creative development relative to the individual's previous creative production. The ultimate educational goal is to have each learner engage over time in increasingly more complex creative practice that eventually has increasing sociocultural value. (p. 3)

This evolving definitional perspective would transition from individualistic to sociocultural contexts at varying times for learners, depending on their individual developmental trajectories. It could occur at a very young age for some learners, or later in the journey of education or life for others: it depends on when their creative outcomes become relevant enough to a field or domain to be assessed by those in those domains for value and originality.

To more accurately nail down these two definitional strands for application to educational practice, we could perhaps further hybridize the definitions of Lubart (2000), Plucker et al. (2004), and Sawyer (2012). The challenge here is to best articulate how the creative output of a group or individual is assessed for degree of novelty or originality. With regards to Sawyer's (2012) individualistic creativity, the word *individualistic* is replaced by the term *personal-historical*, because *personal-historical* could more accurately capture the creative development of an individual or group by comparisons to the previous or historical production of that individual or group. In the context of collaborative creativity, this definitional modification accommodates the creative production of group configurations that are common in mainstream educational practice. Sawyer's (2012) sociocultural strand is augmented with components from Lubart's (2000) definition and the Plucker et al. (2004) definition, with a clearer articulation of the sociocultural context where the degree of novelty or originality of the creative output is compared. The modified definitional strands are as follows:

- **personal-historical creativity:** a sequence of thoughts and actions that leads to novel, adaptive production compared to the previous production of the individual or group
- **sociocultural creativity:** a sequence of thoughts and actions by which an individual or group produces a perceptible product that is both novel and useful as defined within the social context of an established field or domain and its members

The assessment of the degree of novelty or originality of the creative output of an individual or group in educational practice evolves as follows: it starts as historical comparisons of the previous production of the individual or group; it moves to comparisons of creative production in a field or domain, as the creative output of group members grows in sophistication and complexity, and in relevance and importance to the field or domain.

The Concepts of Collaboration and Collaborative Creativity

An examination of a variety of descriptions and definitions of the concept of collaboration from a variety of applied contexts will help shape our understanding of what exactly this term means in applied settings. I can recall sitting in a restaurant meeting with two research assistants regarding work on a previous book when I put forward the necessity to differentiate between the words *collaboration* and *cooperation*, because they are two distinctly different concepts that are easily confused. Right away, one of the assistants googled the words. Cooperation came up as "the process of working together to the same end." Collaboration came up as "the action of working with someone to produce or create something." Each came up as a synonym for the other.

Randy Nelson (2008), former head of Pixar University and currently dean of Apple University, gives a compelling explanation of the difference between these two terms in an online educational video:

> Cooperation for us at Pixar is … a protocol that allows you not to get in each other's way. Think of an assembly line as the quintessential cooperative activity. The guy that puts the fender on at Station 1 has to do a good job. And the lady that puts the headlight on in Station 2—well the guy's job on Station 1 matters. But in a sense, a cooperative enterprise could … be done … by a single person. I put the fender on, and then I walk down here and I put the headlight on. There's nothing about the way Job 1 is done that makes the person doing Job 2 better. [Job 1] can prevent Job 2 from being done as well as it could be done, but there's nothing in the process that's optimizing that. Collaboration has to mean something different. It can't be a synonym for cooperation. Collaboration for Pixar means amplification—the amplification you get by connecting up a bunch of human beings who are listening to each other, interested in each other; who bring separate depth to the problem, bring breadth that gives them interest in the entire solution, [and that] allows them to communicate on multiple different levels, verbally, in writing, in feeling, in acting, in pictures; and in all of those ways, finding the most articulate way to get a high fidelity notion across to a broad range of people so they can each pull on the right lever.

Cooperation among members of a group speaks more to concurrent task completion that may or may not involve interactivity among those involved. Collaboration would appear to speak more to contexts of highly interactive group initiatives, where group members bring complementary skill sets to create potential that was not necessarily attainable by any individual working alone or alongside other individuals. Spitzer (2018) defines collaboration as "being willing and able to blend our ideas and efforts into a communal brain to create better results by working together than by working on our own" (p. 22). This definition emphasizes Nelson's (2008) notion of amplification of others within a group for the purpose of greater creative or problem-resolution potential. Schrage (1990) defines collaboration as the process of shared creation: two or more individuals with complementary skills interacting to create a shared understanding that none had previously possessed or could have come to on their own. Both Spitzer's (2018) and Schrage's (1990) definitions imply a critically important differentiating characteristic of collaboration from cooperation: a truly collaborative environment involves a shift in the disposition of each group member from an ego-centric to a group-centric disposition, or at least a balancing of these dispositions, that ultimately results in shared creative production. In a cooperative dynamic, a participating member does not necessarily have to make this transition to get the task done. Nelson (2008) corroborates this notion.

Several defining attributes emerge to differentiate the concept of collaboration from cooperation. The concept of collaboration would speak to a group of two or more individuals coming together for the purpose co-creating something that didn't exist before, and that was impossible or highly unlikely to accomplish working as individuals. By contrast, cooperation would imply coming together for task completion. This articulation still risks the interpretation that both terms mean the same thing. The ThoughtFarmer (2018) definition of collaboration is simply two or more people working together toward shared goals. This type of basic definition runs a similar risk. It is important to further differentiate these terms by clarifying dispositional attributes of participants in each context. In a collaborative context, Spitzer (2018) and Schrage (1990) imply the ego-centric-to-group-centric shift or balance of group members engaged in shared creation through shared vision, understanding, and/or purpose. Spitzer further qualifies this: "This doesn't mean doing everything as a team or discussing things ad nauseam until complete consensus is reached. It simply means coming together when it adds value and produces better outcomes than we can achieve on our own" (p. 20). Schrage (2015) elaborates on this notion of shared understanding and shared space in the collaborative context:

> Successful collaborators don't just work with each other; they work together through a *shared space*. Shared space—whether physical, virtual or digital—is where collaborators agree to jointly create, manipulate, iterate, capture and critique the *representations of the reality* they seek to discover or design. This holds true for collaboration around products, processes, services, songs, or the exploration of scientific principles. Shared space is the essential means, medium, and mechanism that makes collaboration possible. No shared space? No real collaboration… . Character, cognition, and creativity remain undeniably important. But they play out in the collaborative context of shared spaces where the real work gets done. It takes shared space to create shared understandings. That's the key. (p. 2)

In the collaborative context, creating is a highly interactive process where effective communication is essential. Allison (2015) elaborates on the common principles of this interactivity by adding that group members in a collaborative context should centre around common goals and shared vision, open-mindedness and flexibility, active and deep listening, respect, and trust. Gloor (2017) adds that providing honest feedback among group members is another collaborative interactivity attribute. These attributes of the shared co-creation of a collaborative group are the key differentiating factors from a cooperative context where none of these attributes are necessarily essential for task completion done by two or more individuals.

For this book, collaboration is defined as an adaptation of Schrage (1990): a group of two or more individuals interacting through a shared purpose to produce a shared creation that would be impossible or highly unlikely to produce on their own. Collaboration in this context is characterized by the following attributes:

- The group exists for novel, adaptive creative production.
- The diversity of group members is leveraged toward shared creative production.
- Group members shift from ego-centric to group-centric dispositions to maximize the creative potential of the group.
- The group engages in high-interactivity communication, characterized by open-mindedness, empathy, flexibility, active and deep listening, respect, and honesty.
- The potential creative outcomes of the collaborative group would not be possible, or would be highly unlikely, to achieve as an individual.

The definition of collaborative creativity for the purpose of this book combines the concepts of creativity and collaboration through previously discussed definitional interpretations: a group of two or more individuals with a shared purpose and complementary skills engaged in a sequence of thoughts and actions that leads to novel adaptive production that would be impossible, or highly unlikely, to achieve as individuals.

COLLABORATING TO CREATE 1

Ian Prinsloo on Leveraging Diversity and Brave Spaces

EDITED BY ROBERT KELLY

Ian Prinsloo is a senior consultant with Reos Partners (www.reospartners.com). A creative inquiry facilitator, his work develops the relational quality of groups and makes that interpersonal dynamic the platform for developing innovative solutions to challenges.

Ian has been on the faculty of the Leadership Development program at the Banff Centre in Canada since 2009, designing programs and facilitating custom work for a wide variety of clients. The focus of this work has been the capacity development of leaders to initiate collaborative processes that reframe change as an act of creation. During this time, Ian also ran his own consultancy, working with a wide range of clients across the corporate and nonprofit sector. He has been a regular lecturer with Kaospilot in Denmark since 2011, where he instructs in creative process and the art and craft of being a Kaospilot.

In his previous life, Ian was an award-winning freelance theatre director in Canada. He was artistic director at Theatre Calgary in western Canada for eight years. Ian is a published author on the development of ensemble relationship, metaphoric thinking, and creative process within social change. Helping people connect to their inherent ability to create as the leverage point for change is at the centre of all of Ian's work.

About Collaboration

Jonah Lehrer, author of *Imagine: How Creativity Works*, says that we don't need more creative people, we need to release the creative potential of the people we already have. To me, that's the central goal that active collaboration fulfills. Collaboration requires focus. You collaborate in order to overcome, or realize in some way, some other version of something. So, you are inherently building, creating, developing, if you're collaborating. Collaboration needs to realize the potential of each person involved, so as to maximize potentials—otherwise it isn't true collaboration. In the end, collaboration has to do something, build something, and realize people. It goes beyond the "yes and" culture of accepting every offer from other group members. "Yes and" is how you establish the beginning, the foundation of accepting and growing ideas freely in a culture of collaborative creativity. But once the foundation is set, what you need is another question to push things really far forward, which is: If so, what else is possible? You don't just say "yes and" to suggestions. You think: If that is true, what else is possible? You add to it in that way. "Yes and" is simply confirmatory, and there's only so far confirmation will get you, especially if you're going for a novel adaptation. It is important to establish a safe culture for ideas to flourish, but that is not enough. It is important that collaboration evolves into a brave culture where members are daring and enabled to push the boundaries of creative possibilities.

I think of cooperation as conventional collaboration. It is where those who are leading the process control everything that happens. There is a tremendous amount of agreement among the people who are involved. It's working with your friends, working with people who are like you, working with people who believe the same and have the same worldview, and all those kinds of things. There is control of a lot of the process. A high-control and low-agreement configuration is typical of most classrooms. Students comply because, although they don't agree, they have no way of changing what's happening. Where there's low agreement and low control, or even high agreement and low control, you get into a different type of collaboration. Alignment or shared vision does come with doing things together. But I'd say that, to insist at the very beginning that we all have a shared vision of what we're doing, and what the challenge is, and how we're going to go about it, immediately erodes collaborative potential. To go beyond basic cooperation or conventional collaboration to unleash creative potential, we have to leverage the diversity of the group members.

Leveraging Diversity

When we are leveraging diversity of group members in a collaborative initiative, we have to ask: What's the least number of things people have to agree to in order to work together on the common challenge? So first of all, just because people are diverse doesn't mean they don't all recognize a challenge that they'd like to address. What is the least number of things we have to agree to, so we can begin doing this? How can we maintain maximum diversity, while still moving forward? I think a lot of the time, people think they have to come to agreement on a great number of things that are immaterial to progress. This is one of our biggest social challenges, and often what stymies this process. Why does it have to be that if you don't believe in my worldview, then we can't work together and study? It's not just about finding common ground, it's more about getting rid of distractions that are the assumption of unity. We have this assumption that unity trumps diversity, and that we should be "one in the great oneness," and that this is the highest thing we can ever achieve. This is accompanied by a belief that any sort of friction has to be overcome immediately, instead of letting friction happen and allowing friction to be overcome as people work together. When I used to work in theatre as a director, I often didn't agree with the way some actors approached their craft. I sometimes didn't like the person very much, and sometimes they didn't like me very much, or didn't really buy into what I was doing. But in the end, what they were looking for was a way to address the challenge that was in front of them. We would have to ask: Are the things I'm giving you, and that we are giving each other, moving toward addressing the challenge?

How do we begin to bring members of a group together who are going to address an initiative? It starts with a clear articulation of the challenge, which can substitute for shared vision. This allows the space to leverage the diversity of group members. Then, one of the initial questions is how we can begin leveraging this diversity: How do you release that diversity into a portfolio of initiatives right from the beginning? When I think of directing plays, I worked with individual actors and gave them space to follow their own way to the part and to the play. I allowed for a portfolio of exploration. Again, it always links to the shared challenge that each group member is trying to answer. This is what keeps the collaboration unified. It also means that any questions I ask aren't about whether I think your way is good or not. It's more like, how is your way helping us answer this challenge? The *challenge* exists as the thing to which we are all submitting. When I was directing plays, that's what the play was. You can come up with an idea, but does that help us realize this play? It's about how an idea works in relationship with the overall structure.

When leveraging diversity, we have to look at how diversity will play out within the dynamic of a collaborative group. Leveraging diversity specifically points to the balance between self and group. What is it like to travel back and forth between these polarities? What is like to balance the assertion of an individual's ideas and a commitment to the unity of the group? At the beginning, when a group comes together, there is diversity, and that means different ideas about how we approach things. Split out: start doing those different ideas and see what you discover. Split into smaller units. Within a smaller unit, I can have an identity. It's important for me to have my own identity within that smaller group—again, to leverage that diversity. I can be both outside the larger group, and unified to it. This allows group members to move back and forth: to assert what they believe, in relationship to others, and still be connected to the larger group. The idea is to exercise our will to assert ourselves, while having a will to unify with others, and developing a way to continually move back and forth between these wills.

It can get played up as a negative thing, when individuals are perceived to be asserting themselves too much. Often going unnoticed in collaboration is the person who always aligns with the group. They are always doing unity, unity, unity, unity, above all else, without ever asserting themselves. These people need to assert themselves in a collaborative context. If they don't exercise assertion, they are not realizing their potential or the group's potential. Without assertion, their potential is clouded by everyone else: they become invisible.

Brave Spaces

Safe spaces are great at the beginning of this process. However, if we're going to do something really challenging and interesting, things have to move beyond safe to get daring—more daring than high risk. The collaborative space has to become a brave space. Take 4-year-old children, for example: they take risks all the time, because they just have no concept of what's going to happen. Risk in this context is inherently something that is dangerous and not well thought out. By contrast, being daring means that I actually understand the risk, I have skills and abilities, and I'm moving to the very edge of what those are in this situation, and possibly beyond the edge. From my theatre experience, I have witnessed actors on stage who were daring, heavily invested in what they were doing, revealing something new as they explored. It was not accidental. They trusted where they were going. It's about recognizing the moment where we realize that being in a safe space is no longer going to get us where we need to go. We now need to go to a brave space, where the unity of the group is not as important as the friction that comes with diversity in the face of a challenge, realizing that diversity is necessary in the face of a challenge. However, this doesn't come without its conflicts and disagreements. This is where deep and active listening comes in, to enable understanding, trust, and empathy to emerge. The group becomes like a family. That is part of being in a brave space. I know that if, for some reason, you hurt me in some way, or I hurt you, we're going to both stay in the space, to actually engage with that. What you assume with a family is that your family's going to stick around to work out the hurt.

Don McIntyre on the Gifting Economy, an Indigenous Perspective on Collaboration

EDITED BY ROBERT KELLY

Don McIntyre is an Ojibway of the Wolf Clan from Timiskaming First Nation. He has been adopted into the Potlatch by the Beaver Clan of the Nisga'a.

Don is presently assistant professor in the Dhillon School of Business at the University of Lethbridge. He is also ongoing faculty at the Banff Centre in the Indigenous Leadership and Management Development programs. Don has taught at colleges, universities, and in First Nation communities in North America and around the world. He has consulted in the areas of Indigenous art and traditions, social innovation, law and society, negotiations, and Treaty.

Don is a recognized painter and carver who has worked throughout his life in the traditional style of the Anishinabe, which the Anishinabe have practised on their Traditional Territory for generations. More recently, he has incorporated many Haida teachings and modern urban-life visions into his work. He has travelled and exhibited artwork in a spectrum of media and themes around the world.

The Gifting Economy

From my traditional understanding of the world, an Anishinaabek perspective, we come from and continue to maintain a gifting economy. A gifting economy resonates in many ways with the concept of a collaborative culture, where everyone looks out for everyone else; there is a reciprocal expectation. The primary idea, central to the concept of a gifting economy, is that we, as individuals, don't own anything. By this, I mean that all that I have is a gift, and my responsibility to the gifts I have received is to share them. The word *Anishinaabek* means "good humans." In a gifting economy, people say, "We don't own it. It's not ours. We're happy to share it with you. It was given to us and it is our responsibility to pass it on to help it build something bigger and better. Our community becomes better by showing how much we can give away." This is how we become "good humans."

The gifting economy is created with the idea that I give away everything I have, and that I'm completely entrenched in an economy where everybody thinks I am most valuable because I give away the most. Everybody around me wants to improve their value, and they do it in an opposite way to a Western context, where I'm going to improve my value by maybe getting a bigger house, or a better car, and all of these things that I keep. In a gifting economy, I give away as much as I can, and people respond with, "Look at how much that person gave away. I have to prove that I'm as worthy as him, so I'm going to give away even more." Within the system, people are only ever without for a very limited time, because, almost immediately, others that are part of the system will reciprocate my sharing. I witness this sensibility all the time with Elders. Elders are very willing to share their knowledge. There is a sense of responsibility to pass their knowledge on. Individuals attempt to return the gifts of Elders in the form of sacred medicines, food, or material objects. When Elders attend gatherings and there is a giveaway, they will be compensated for the many gifts they have given. At Potlatches or powwows, a lot of blankets, tea, sugar, clothing, art, cash, and many other items will be shared with the witnesses. Everyone accepts what they are given and they use what they need. But when you go into an Elder's back room, you will see that the Elder has got a very large number of blankets and other items from the gatherings. However, it is not hoarding in a Western sense, because they're gathering to give it all away. They're just waiting for the opportunity.

Historically, with the arrival of the commodified economy, European settlers and government Indian agents saw the West Coast Peoples engaging in their Potlatch ceremonies and saw the giveaway observances of the Eastern Nations, and they outlawed these economic systems. The anti-Potlatch provisions of the Indian Act[1] in Canada were basically the government saying "you are not allowed to give anything away anymore," because, from a Western perspective, there was no way to survive by giving away. In a Western system, one cannot live without gathering and hoarding and having the most, which is the opposite way of being in the world from a gifting economy.

The gifting way of being is a relationship between the person receiving the gift and the person giving the gift and the gift itself. Part of the responsibility of that relationship is to continue to move the gifts, and that includes all of the gifts, not just the gifts that I pass on, but the gifts that you have. Importantly, you have to enhance, and also advance, the story of the gifts to explain why I gave you the gift and what the circumstances were.

The Importance of Story

One of the major stories, about the genesis of gifting, comes from the Creator, Gitchi-Manitou. Gitchi-Manitou gave gifts to all of the nations. Among the animal nations—the two-leggeds, four-leggeds, wingeds, and swimmers—special powers and natures were conferred to the winged nations and to the water beings. To the plant beings was given a spirit of life, growth, healing, and beauty. Humans were made last of all. To us was provided the greatest gift—the power to dream.

> Kitche Manitou then made The Great Laws of Nature for the well-being and harmony of all things and all creatures. The Great Laws governed the place and movement of sun, moon, earth, and stars; governed the powers of wind, water, fire, and rock; governed the rhythm and continuity of life, birth, growth, and decay. All things lived and worked by these laws.
>
> Kitche Manitou had brought into existence his vision.[2]

All the nations have gifts that they continue to give to all the other nations. Every being walks into relationships with all of the other nations, to ensure that food, shelter, oxygen, and all things necessary for life are available to all living things. With the gift of dreaming, what humans are supposed to do is dream up how all of these can be used to work together, to work in relationship with each other. This is the Great Law.

The gifting system has worked for more than ten thousand years. It falls apart when one person says, "I take your gifts and I'm just going to put them in my pocket, keep them for my own. I'm not going to share. I'm not going to feel responsible. I don't care that I have no value in the gifting economy, because I have more material stuff than anybody." As soon as one person removes themselves from responsibility to the whole, the system falls apart. As soon as the system becomes individuals taking ownership and denying responsibility to the community, appropriation begins because you're not telling the story of where credit is due.

From a traditional Anishinaabek perspective, traditional education is about experiential learning. It's about creating building blocks and it's constantly about the story. From the time you are just a very young baby, you are told the stories of Creation and the Ancestors. The stories get told at family gatherings. They get told at bedtime. They get told in the winter. Your responsibility, when a baby, is to listen to the stories. When you have heard enough, you sleep. You get used to the language. As you grow older and stay awake longer, the stories become more in-depth; new aspects and pieces get added to them. Toddlers and young children are responsible to gather the information they need to fit into the world. The stories are told in greater detail. The same story that used to take five minutes, takes 50 minutes. Then as an adult, that same story may take five days, as more is added, and your responsibility to the community is to use that story to share the gifts the Creator has given to you. Some hunt and share the bounty. Some become political warriors. And some become Traditional Knowledge Holders. Older adults are responsible for educating the younger ones who share their propensities.

Finally, Elders are responsible for ensuring the story perseveres. That same story that was the beginning point teaches how to hunt, harvest, create, and socialize. Eventually all the teachings and learnings from all the stories become the social contract that is the Great Law of the Anishinaabek system.

We continually refer back to those very, very basic stories to express the most complex of ideas. Nobody owns those. Ownership among the Anishinaabek is different than the Western idea. Nobody can own the stories. Knowledge wants to be free, but there are people who are responsible for those stories. And those people must be taken care of by the rest of the community. This is the reciprocal expectation of the system. In the Western system, we look at ownership as a bundle of rights. I have the right to deny every person. I have the right to make money from what I own and the right to enjoy it. From an Indigenous perspective, rather than a bundle of rights, we have a bundle of responsibilities. Those responsibilities are to the gifts that we have received from the Creator, the gifts that we've received from other people in our community, and the gifts we've received from other nations. Responsibility demands that I tell you the story of why I am responsible, why my family is responsible, and why my great-grandchildren will be responsible.

Art, the Story, and the Way Forward

A lot of the perception of Indigenous culture has been defined by Western perspectives and Western law. The Canadian Constitution[3] defines who qualifies as an Aboriginal, and the Indian Act[4] determines what Aboriginals can and cannot do. This is who I am, this is what I do, this is how my government is organized, and all of those things. But I still hold those sacred stories and those sacred ways of being that are Indigenous, that are precontact. They never actually disappeared, no matter how hard the residential schools attempted to make them disappear. They didn't. The language didn't disappear. Now the process is to revitalize them. For that reason, as artist and teacher, I'm happy to share those stories within both systems. If I share my story, if I share my technique, you have to be willing to take it the way that it was given. It was given for you to pass on, not for you to hoard and profit from.

I paint in an Ojibway style. Part of my responsibility as an Aboriginal, as a contemporary Aboriginal man, is to ensure that that style, those forms as ways of communicating information, are continued in a contemporary context. My Uncles describe the practice of Indigenous art forms as "showing the world through Ojibway eyes." When I paint or carve, those methods of communicating stories are equivalent to a literary written form of the West. Often it is said by the courts and in education curriculums that Indigenous people come from an oral tradition and that they had no writing. I was taught this is a falsehood. Indigenous Peoples had written forms of communication. They don't look like Western constructs of writing. Contemporary Aboriginal Peoples practise these Indigenous forms as our responsibility to our communities, our Nations, and the world at large. My painting style tells those same basic stories in a contemporary context. Using the Indigenous forms allows those stories to be told in a much more nuanced way. I can paint one painting: I can show that painting to toddlers and tell the five-minute story, or show that same painting to a university class to tell the 50-minute story. I hope to one day be able to show that painting and tell that story over five days. I just don't know enough yet.

Education

There are many things that the Western system superimposed on Indigenous awareness that were largely opposite to the Indigenous way of being. Education is one of these areas. The imposed Western construct invalidated the idea that there was a level of responsibility, that education could be experiential, that education could be based on building blocks, that education could be a collaborative, creative process. It said education has to be in a desk. Education has to look like it did in Europe. It has to look like the structures put in place during the Industrial Revolution. This system of education was not about making good humans, but rather about making good factory workers. During the Residential School period,[5] Indigenous children were told not to speak their languages, never to question, only to answer when asked, and only in English or French. Sit, listen, and regurgitate what you were told.

The Indigenous perspective on education is very different from a Western outlook. It's a system that says: question everything. It is necessary to talk about the story and the lessons because it's all situational. One individual may see a situation differently than another because they're coming at it from different backgrounds, ages, and potentially a different space. It is necessary to respect the educational journey each individual is on, as you never know where or how their gifts will manifest. Every member of the Anishinabe system is to be honoured for their knowledge and perspective. My work in the area of Indigenous Trans-systemics fits perfectly into education. It advocates for recognition of other ways of knowing and all ways of teaching. The Anishinabe way of teaching and learning starts with the telling of the very basic story. This is the foundation upon which all knowledge is based. Pieces are added to the story as individuals graduate to deeper enquiries, and activities are added to bring them closer to understanding and manifesting their roles within the community as good humans. For example, once you know the story of Elk, you will be shown how to draw Elk. This allows you to be taught how to pray to Elk for the gifts Elk offer (like food), at which time you can be taught to hunt Elk in a good way. Each piece is a building block to new experiences and knowledge. Our religion, our education, our social construct, our laws, all of those are tied together into one giant package that is us striving to be good humans. It's about recognizing the responsibilities we have to our Nation, our community, and ourselves.

NOTES

1 The federal government banned the Potlatch from 1884 to 1951 through an amendment to the Indian Act. The government and its supporters saw these ceremonies as preventing the assimilation of Indigenous populations, and as anti-Christian and reckless and wasteful of personal property.

2 Basil Johnston, *Ojibway Heritage* (Toronto: McClelland and Stewart, 1976), 13.

3 The Constitution Act, 1982, defines Aboriginals as Indians, Métis, and Inuit under Section 35.

4 Indian Act, R.S.C 1985, C 1-5.

5 The Residential School system was officially in place from 1830 until 1996.

2

The Transformative Dynamics of a New Educational Ecosystem

The Need for Educational Transformation: Adapting to Rapid Sociocultural and Technological Change

The understanding of collaborative creativity established in Chapter 1 leads to the question of how this concept works in educational practice, from early childhood to higher education, in both relevance and application. This chapter examines the dynamics of change in educational, sociocultural, technological, and economic contexts that are necessary to a new way of being educationally in the world. These transformative dynamics inform both the macro and micro perspectives of educational practice for wholesale transformation to an educational ecosystem built around collaborative creativity, as opposed to incremental retrofitting of traditional educational discourses informed by an industrial model that is decades, perhaps centuries, old. Change is inevitable and constant. We have to adapt to change and create positive change. Former Columbia University president Nicholas Butler said it best when he described "the three kinds of people in the world." There are the few who make things happen, the many more who watch things happen, and the overwhelming majority who have no notion of what is happening. He further adds the importance of the masses in the third group to aspire to be in the first group through education. This chapter views the way forward as embracing transformative dynamics proactively to effect positive change through collaborative creativity.

In the introduction, "Collaborative Creativity: A Match Made in Heaven, Desperately Needed on Earth," we can see from OECD's Education 2030 initiative and the United Nations' Sustainable Development Goals that fundamental change for educational practice is a necessity because of the growing complexity of the diverse problems and design challenges that face us today. Change is also needed for the anticipated complexity of problems and design challenges that haven't emerged yet in any number of sectors. Allison (2015) emphasizes that emerging problems in this sea of change are growing in complexity, and that dealing with these problems will require a whole new approach. He stresses that a lot of the existing problem-solving approaches embedded in organizational cultures are not flexible or agile enough to deal with this emerging, evolving, complex problem-solving. Because of exponentially increasing connectivity, a collaborative group or network can recruit and engage diverse resources and databases to deal with these complexities for the advance of design and creative potentials, and ultimately problem resolutions—potentials and resolutions that wouldn't emerge from individuals or small groups working in isolation.

Waks (2014) and Cheek (2015) contend that traditional educational discourses, focused largely on the dissemination of discipline data and the requisite recall and restating of this data as an indicator of educational success, have become largely obsolete and irrelevant given the backdrop of constant sociocultural and technological change. These traditional educational discourses are characterized by student and educator dispositions that are largely passive, consumption intense, and competitive. This results in educational cultures that rely heavily on learner compliance and cooperation for task completion. Educator and learner socialization within these cultures breeds mistrust, social isolation, teaching and learning for assessment, risk aversion, reliance on extrinsic motivation, and fear and anxiety (Kelly, 2016). This socialization reaches very deeply into the foundational beliefs of educators and learners about what education is, making change, and ultimately educational transformation, very difficult. Rapid sociocultural and technological change necessitates a complete transformation of educational practice that goes well beyond applying an innovative bandage of new trends and ideas onto traditional educational discourses: it necessitates a completely new sensibility and way of doing that is centred around the concept of collaborative creativity. Bringing change to traditional discourses in education is extremely difficult, because it requires overcoming the inertia of decade after decade of traditional ways of doing. Government initiatives at various jurisdictional levels that are responsible for developing curricula across the age and discipline spectrum become risk averse when it comes to advancing profound educational change, because ultimately they are accountable to electorates whose educational sensibilities reflect their own educational histories that are typically steeped in traditional discourses.

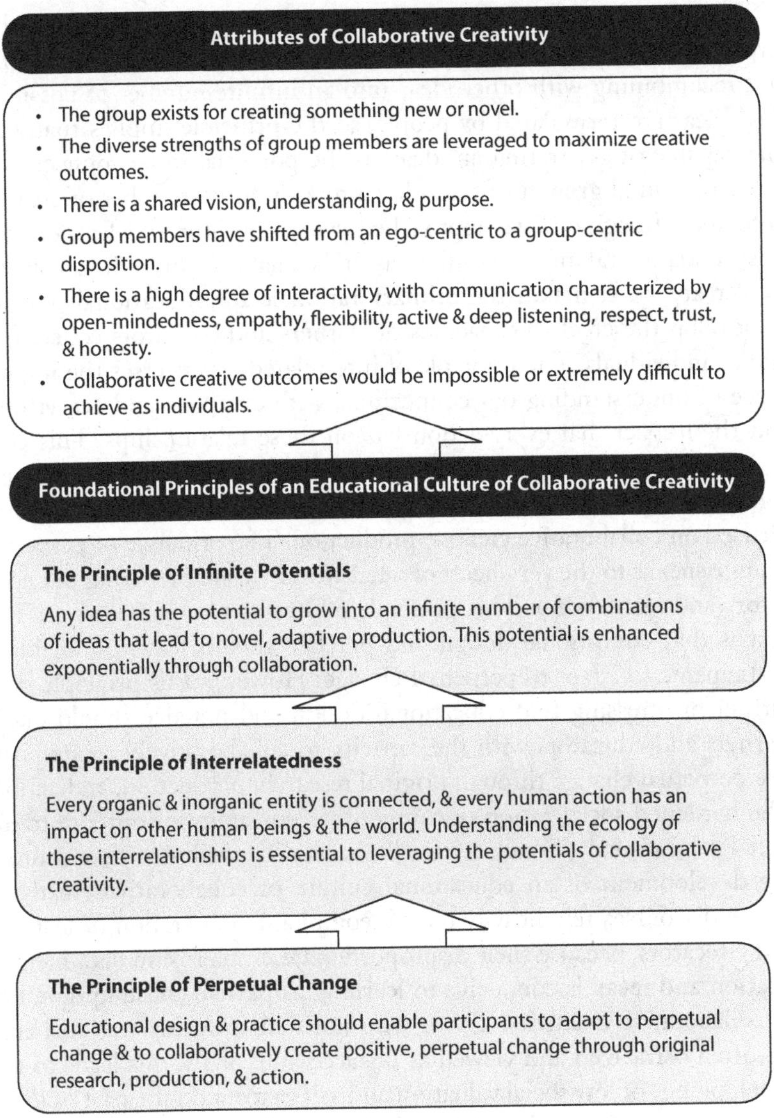

FIGURE 1. Foundational principles and attributes of collaborative creativity

In *Creative Development: Transforming Education through Design Thinking, Innovation, and Invention* (Kelly, 2016), I describe three foundational principles that inform an educational culture of collaborative creativity. Figure 1 shows these foundational principles in relation to the attributes of collaborative creativity.

The principle of infinite potentials is built around the belief that any idea has the potential to grow exponentially through combining and recombining with other ideas into an infinite number of possibilities. Ideas are formulated by people, so the principle implies that anyone capable of generating an idea has the potential to be connected to the exponential growth of that idea into an infinite number of creative outcomes. Imagine if we approached every educator and learner with this fundamental understanding as it is enabled through collaborative creativity. It makes the primary rationale for educational practice to develop the creative capacities of learners and educators collectively and as individuals. The principle of interrelatedness stresses the importance of understanding our connections with everyone and everything, and the impact that every action has on these relationships. This ecological perspective is essential to create the basis for sensitive, empathic communication that creates cultures of trust and honesty, and networks focused on collaborative creative production. The principle of perpetual change speaks to the very heart of what world we are preparing our educators and learners for. This principle addresses two perspectives. The first is that educational design and practice should focus on enabling participants to adapt to perpetual change. However, this principle goes further by stressing that educational design and practice should equip learners and educators with the capacity to collaboratively create positive perpetual change through original research, production, and action. The hardened socialization of competitive, consumption-intense traditional educational discourses instills hardened attributes that counter the development of an educational culture of collaborative creativity. These discourses rely heavily on the compliant cooperation of learners and educators, because their disproportionate emphasis on data memorization and recall is conducive to learning as passive consumption, not as collaborative creativity. Those who don't fit into this way of being are often ostracized and viewed as unsuccessful. Sadly, this leads to the development of low social valuation and self-esteem on the part of these learners, when in actual fact these individuals have unlimited inventive potential and, for the most part, function within what most would consider the realm of normal human beings. Many school initiatives at the forefront of creativity in education featured in my 2012 book *Educating for Creativity: A Global Conversation* are testimony to this: their impetus for coming into existence was to reengage learners that had become alienated from the predominant traditional discourse.

Educational transformation will require resocialization, or Benammar's (2012) concept of reframing, where all of our traditional beliefs about education and ways of doing have to be questioned and analyzed from the perspective of relevance to adapting to rapid change and creating positive change. This requires letting go of dated and obsolete educational practices, and overcoming the inertia that perpetuates these practices, to enable the embracing of new ways of doing. Futurist Alvin Toffler put it this way in 1970 in *Future Shock*: "illiteracy" in the 21st century will not refer to the skills of reading and writing, but to the inability to learn, unlearn, and relearn. Collaborative creativity is at the very core of this educational transformation.

From Consume to Create: The Foundational Dynamics Informing Educational Transformation

There are several transformational dynamics that help inform and shape an educational culture of collaborative creativity. These transformational dynamics are influenced by predicted future responses to trends, but more importantly by prognostications about the evolution of sociocultural and technological change, and how our way of being in the world must adapt to this rapid change. Benammar, van Dijk, and Wolfe (2014) describe trends as measurable tendencies that shift our reality, are based on fact, and are measurable. They further define a paradigm as a way of being in the world based on fact and observation. Figure 2 shows the comprehensive transformative dynamics at play in an educational shift toward a culture of collaborative creativity. These transformative dynamics reinterpret and combine concepts described by Benammar et al. (2014) from the THNK School of Creative Leadership in Amsterdam; Prince, Saveri, and Swanson (2015) from KnowledgeWorks on navigating the future of learning; Saveri and Chwierut (2011) from the Institute for the Future on the future of learning agents; Scharmer (2018), and Scharmer and Kaufer (2013), on adapting to the future; and my own work (Kelly, 2012, 2016) on the concept of creative development. These transformative dynamics revolve around three core dynamics: consume to create, passive to interactive, and authoritative to empowering. They are accompanied by complimentary interrelated dynamics that collectively transform current educational culture into a culture of collaborative creativity.

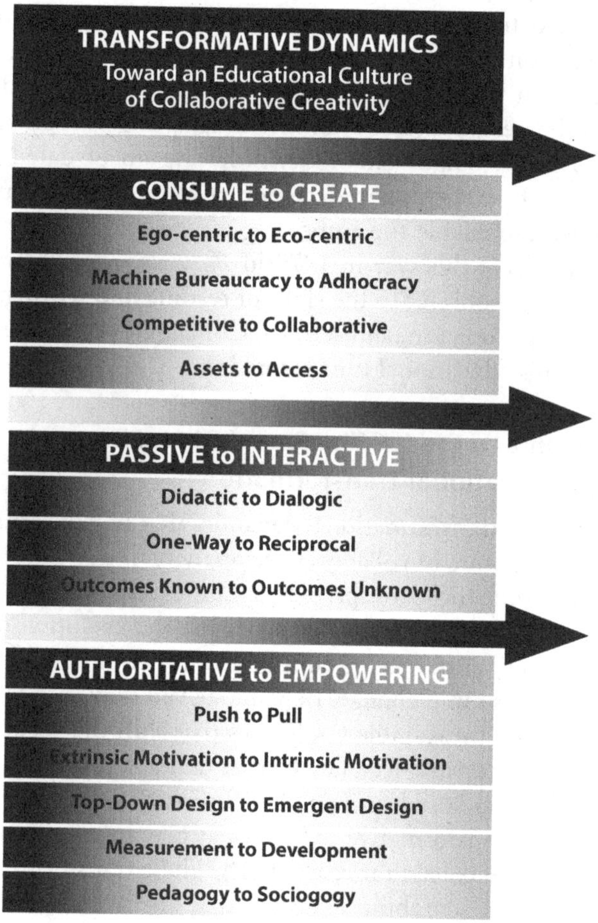

FIGURE 2. Transformative dynamics that inform change toward an educational culture of collaborative creativity

Consume to Create, and Ego-centric to Eco-centric

A primary transformational dynamic described by Benammar et al. (2014) is *consume to create*. Transformative dynamics were originally articulated in the context of innovation in business and entrepreneurship. Their implications for transformation in education are quite profound. The transformative dynamic of *consume to create* is central to the belief that education exists not just to equip learners with content knowledge of diverse disciplines, but also to instill an innate dispositional capacity for collaborative creativity that enables the application of discipline knowledge and processes to innovations for the benefit of others. I raised the question in Kelly (2016): What is the purpose of equipping learners with discipline content knowledge if we don't simultaneously equip them with creative capacity, including the tools, processes, tactics, and strategies to collaboratively innovate through original research, production, and action? These are not mutually exclusive concepts. Developing creative capacity does not preclude the enhancement of discipline content knowledge. In fact, it provides a relevant and meaningful context for acquiring discipline content knowledge. However, a disproportionate emphasis on the dissemination and memorization of discipline content knowledge, as accepted mainstream educational practice, leads to an educational culture that is fundamentally consumption intense. We get good at what we practice the most. Learners and educators engaged in this traditional educational discourse largely practise the dissemination of discipline content knowledge, and the memorization and the restatement of this knowledge. This system is basically focused on instilling data in students. Assessment is largely built around the measurement of a learner's capacity to retain and restate the mandatory curriculum content built around a growing discipline knowledge. Longitudinal success in this context is viewed like this: the more knowledge one has, the more successful one is (Nair, 2014). One cannot make the assumption that a high level of discipline content knowledge automatically confers a high creative capacity. Increasing discipline competency is a necessary contributing factor that enables high creative capacity, but high creative capacity comes from engagement in the processes, tactics, and strategies of increasingly sophisticated creative practice, not consumption-intense educational practice. A consumption-intense educational culture does not equip educators and learners with the creative capacity and enabling collaborative culture to deal with evolving sociocultural, economic, and technological challenges. Transforming from an educational consumption-intense disposition to a creativity-intense disposition is an essential, central transformational dynamic for educational practice.

Scharmer and Kaufer (2013) describe the predominant dispositions as "ego-centric" while arguing for the need to transition to an ecological sensibility or "eco-system":

> When operating with ego-system awareness, we are driven by the concerns and intentions of our small ego self. When operating with eco-system awareness we are concerned with the concerns and intentions...informed by the well-being of the whole. (p. 2)

They further emphasize the importance of this shift:

> This shift in awareness from ego-system to eco-system is something that we are approaching and living through not only as groups

> and organizations, but also as a global community. Pioneering the principles and personal practices that help us to perform this shift may well be one of the most important undertakings of our time. (p. 2)

This resonates with a foundational attribute of a culture of collaborative creativity: the transition of group members from an ego-centric disposition to a group-centric disposition, which allows groups to truly leverage the strengths of each contributing member for a collaborative creative outcome that would be impossible, or highly unlikely, to achieve as an individual. The shift from *ego-centric* to *eco-* or *group-centric* is essential in the shift from *consume* to *create*, or more precisely the shift from *consume* to *collaboratively create*.

Machine Bureaucracy to Adhocracy

Consumption in a traditional educational sense requires learners to be compliant and cooperative. It requires learners to be attentive listeners. In this educational environment, these attributes are essential for success, but they are a far cry from the dispositional attributes needed to be a full participant in an educational culture of collaborative creativity. Typical educational organizational structures resonate with Mintzberg's (1989) machine bureaucracy. Standardized curricula and standardized assessments ensure that the system is functioning properly, and that students are achieving and educators are teaching to preset standards. The architecture of an organizational structure built around standardization, and its corresponding pedagogical and assessment practices, precludes true transformation to a culture of creativity, because it is rooted in standardization from the ground up, and not in collaborative innovation and invention. Typical educational cultures are highly competitive because of assessment by peer comparison. They are also largely passive because they foster the mass-compliance and cooperative dispositions that enable them to exist. This is not to say that educators and educational jurisdictions have not introduced wave after wave of perceived innovative and transformational educational initiatives to improve the educational experience for learners. Inquiry-based learning, personalized learning, project-based learning, makerspaces, and experiential learning, to name a few, are initiatives that have been introduced over time into the standardization matrix. Waks (2014) contends that because of the inertia of the fundamental machine bureaucracy focused on standardization, these well-intended practices lose their most transformative properties. On their own, they are often viewed in terms of educational ideals, but when retrofitted onto a system built around standardization, they become subservient to this culture rather than transformative. This "skew" effect from the inertia of traditional educational discourse happens time and time again.

The transformation of education into a culture of collaborative creativity requires a very different organizational structure that is built around creative production through innovation and invention. Mintzberg's (1989) "adhocracy" is an example of an innovative organizational structure designed around creative production. Mintzberg says that "sophisticated innovation requires a very different configuration, one that is able to fuse experts drawn from different disciplines into smoothly functioning ad hoc project teams" (p. 199). Tharp (2009) elaborates on the nature of adhocracy as an organization type built around creativity:

> Adhocratic organizations value flexibility, adaptability, and thrive in what would have earlier been viewed as unmanageable chaos. High-tech companies like Google are prototypical Create (adhocracy) organizations. Google develops innovative web tools, taking advantage of entrepreneurial software engineers and cutting-edge processes and technologies. Their ability to quickly develop new services and capture market share has made them leaders in the marketplace and forced less nimble competition to play catch-up. (p. 3)

The primary organizational referent for most educational practice from kindergarten to higher education is the machine bureaucracy. To most, it is the only viable educational organizational structure because it is the only structure they have ever known. Mintzberg (1989) relates that *structure* in this culture means "hierarchy of authority, top-down control, unity of command, detailed planning, formalization of procedure... . Adhocracy which violates every one of these notions looks like chaos, like the absence of structure" (p. 197). It *looks* like chaos, but really the opposite is true. Allison (2015) emphasizes that the increasing complexity of emerging problems requires new approaches beyond traditional machine bureaucracies that lack the flexibility and agility to deal with growing complexity. The adhocratic organizational structure tends to be a flattened structure with rotating leadership. The rotating leadership is partially dependent on required expert resources, which resonates with Gloor's (2017) rotating leadership as an honest signal of collaboration and an indicator of higher creative potentials in a group. The adhocratic group can be amorphous: the required expertise and diverse inputs toward design and problem resolution come and go as needed.

The adhocratic organizational structure, built around creative production with a high degree of flexibility and adaptability, has a very complex structure that is mutable by nature. It is not chaotic or lacking in structure: it is highly organized in highly complex ways.

The challenge facing educators and educational administrators wishing for true educational change, transformation, and innovation is how to circumvent the deeply entrenched sensibility of the machine bureaucracy to create an organizational adhocratic space that exists for creative production and innovation for both educators and learners. The overriding raison d'être of traditional educational discourses, centred on standardization, precludes or reduces the transformative effect of these initiatives.

Machine bureaucracies are innately risk averse. I was recently involved in a government-initiated curriculum redesign for every discipline from K to 12. We were placed in discipline design groups and were given the task of redesigning the curriculum in that area under the guidance of government curriculum leaders. I made a suggestion at the onset of the design process to the leader of our discipline area: "Shouldn't we be designing the curriculum for over the horizon?" My thought was that these curriculum redesign initiatives happen infrequently, and the reality of rapid sociocultural and technological change meant we should design the most progressive, forward-thinking curriculum possible based on available research and input from leaders in the discipline fields. The response I got was that we should be designing for this side of the horizon because of potential implementation issues with the general public. I certainly understand the concern of governments around voter accountability. However, I felt that we were obligated to lead and my response was: "Why don't we design for over the horizon and design an innovative implementation strategy?" In other words, let's view any perceived implementation issues as a design constraint. We were, after all, supposedly functioning as a design team. Needless to say, the inertia of the established culture of standardization of the machine bureaucracy won out, precluding incredible innovative potentials of curriculum development. As a design team, we didn't exist for pure innovation and invention, but rather for compliance and cooperation, and for minor collaborative creativity within limited ranges and a standardized format that precluded any major innovative leap.

Machine bureaucracy organizational structure and adhocratic organizational structure, despite being fundamental opposites, are not mutually exclusive operationally. Educational administrators and innovative educators must create spaces within organizations for adhocracies to exist without the constraints of the predominant culture. These adhocratic subcultures or parallel cultures within organizations should be allowed to create, invent, and innovate, and ultimately to lead. Truly transformative innovation in education is very limited, if not impossible, otherwise. Organizations and corporate entities must have the courage and the foresight to engage in self-disruptive innovation: they must aim constantly to reinvent and adapt to rapid change, while constantly questioning foundational premises that previously informed their structure and corresponding practices.

An issue that arises in birthing adhocratic subcultures or parallel cultures focused on collaborative creative production within organizations is finding professionals and experts to populate these cultures. A high level of knowledge expertise in one or more disciplines does not equate with high levels of collaborative or creative attributes. If one's only educational experience has been functioning in a machine bureaucracy culture of standardization, then it is not a given that one has the dispositional depth needed for collaborative creativity. Collaborative creativity is not the primary rationale of the predominant educational culture. It is absolutely essential in going forward that, if adhocratic organizational spaces for collaborative creativity are created, the professional participants in these spaces have the tactics, strategies, and dispositional development to enable maximal creative outcomes. This could go as far as engaging in resocialization or reframing, where each participant questions their way of knowing and being to enable the flexibility that allows adaption to the salient features of a creative culture that doesn't share the attributes of what they are used to. This forms the basis of a very compelling argument about teacher education: K to 12 educators, and teaching and learning initiatives among faculty in higher education, need deliberate engagement with formal dispositional development embracing the theory, practice, tactics, and strategies of collaborative creativity. This has been the central rationale for the growth and development of the graduate programs in education that I designed and direct, which are focused on collaborative creativity and are featured in Chapter 5, "Giant Lobsters, Whales, and Elephants: A Case Study in Developing an Educational Culture of Collaborative Creativity."

Passive to Interactive

Benammar et al. (2014) elaborate on the dynamic of *consume to create* by describing a subdynamic of *passive to active*. A benchmark dispositional attribute of an educational culture of collaborative creativity is its high degree of interactivity. This speaks to the fundamental nature of dispositional change from a consumption-intense educational discourse to an educational culture of collaborative creativity. Predominant curriculum and pedagogical design, built around traditional educational discourses, are mostly conducive to passive learner dispositions. Often the architectural design of educational institutions supports these traditional discourses. Nair (2014), and Nair and Doctori (2019), describe this architecture as "cells and bells," capturing its didactic expert-to-novice delivery and sage-on-the-stage sensibility. A transition built around the consume-to-create dynamic toward an educational culture of collaborative creativity requires a shift from the traditional predominant passive learner disposition to a disposition built around interactivity. Collaboration by its very nature is interactivity intense. This high level of interactivity is necessitated by the constant need for idea exchange and development, and prototype development and refinement, so that collaborative creative production can realize its greatest potential. It is a sad statement on educational practice that learners and educators in traditional educational discourses can be located in classrooms in close physical proximity for several months of a semester or academic year without any meaningful exchange of ideas for the purpose of creative production. The logic behind making students physically attend academic lectures of one to two hours, in classes whose size can balloon to the hundreds, is highly questionable. This passive, didactic orientation can easily be replaced by a recorded lecture with accompanying transcript and access for expert clarification, which learners could review outside of formal class time. Students could examine the content in digestible bites that suit their learning, so their actual class time could be spent in meaningful interactivity with colleagues engaging in collaborative creativity. This "flipped classroom" concept has been around for quite awhile, yet traditional mass lectures still persist. I find nothing worse in teacher education than when I hear a complaint from a frustrated education student who just got out of two-hour lecture delivered to a class of five hundred on the topic of student-centred learning. If they talk about it, why don't they practise it? This counterintuitive phenomenon of "do as I say, not as I do" is not lost on any student of any age. It is a classic premise for learner dissociation.

Didactic to Dialogic, and One-Way to Reciprocal

The transformational dynamic *didactic to dialogic* amplifies the passive-to-interactive dynamic by emphasizing active and deep listening for the purpose of generative interaction serving collaborative creative

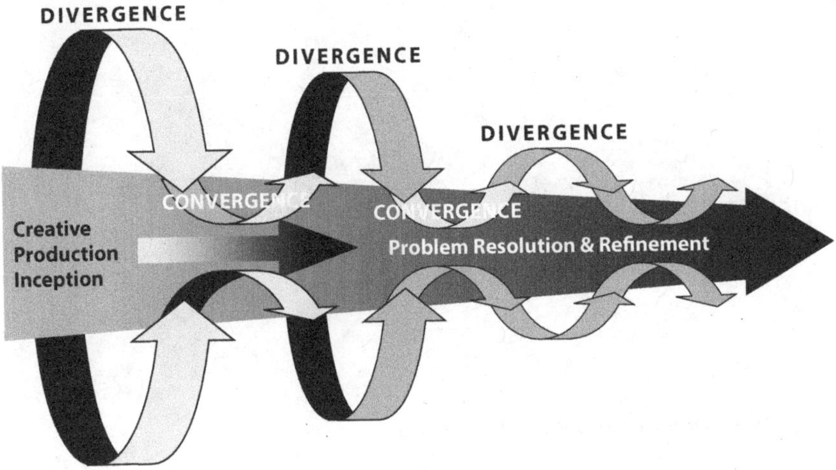

FIGURE 3. The generative divergent-convergent pulse of ideation and prototyping in design practice over time, from creative production inception to problem resolution and refinement

production, as opposed to passive listening for the sole purpose of knowledge retention or cooperation for task completion. It is supported by another transformational dynamic of *one-way to reciprocal*, which is communicative reciprocity among educators and learners that grows from the need, in an interactivity-intense educational environment, to transform learners from passive consumers to co-authors, co-designers, co-creators, and co-producers, as well as initiators, of innovation and invention alongside educators and experts. This need for reciprocal relationships in educational environments that are highly interactive to enable a culture of collaborative creativity becomes clearer on examining the collaborative design process, with its iterations of idea generation and prototyping of creative outcomes over time.

IDEO (2012) describes the design process as five stages: discovery, interpretation, ideation, experimentation, and evolution. Discovery is viewed as the initial stage of framing and preparing the problem, followed by a second stage focused on how to interpret the problem. The generation of ideas, and experimentation through prototyping, for problem resolution follow as the third and fourth stages. The fifth stage, evolution, is focused on the continued refinement and further development of prototypes. This approach to describing the design process has an affinity with the stage theory of creativity described in Chapter 1. Figure 3 illustrates the design process as a series of iterations of *divergent*

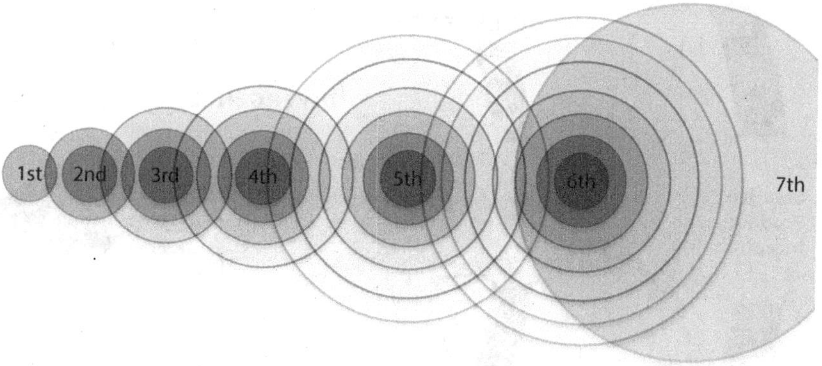

FIGURE 4. Ideation hybridization waves

generation of ideas and *convergent* development of prototypes toward the refinement of the problem resolution.

Smith (1998) describes idea generation as the indispensable core of creativity. Idea generation encompasses not only the generation of new ideas as pure thought in the imaginative realm, but also the generation of ideas through experimentation, by developing prototypes in the currency of the discipline where the creative production is occurring. In an educational context, the growth and development of ideas leading to creative production does not happen in isolation. Creative production through the design process involves an incredible amount of fuel, which is the constant flow of ideas either to instigate new creative directions or as part of continuous feedback spirals directed at the refinement of prototypes. At the onset of a design sequence, it is critical to have a large quantity of ideas flowing in. It is equally critical to have a steady influx of new ideas throughout the design process to maximize prototyping and refinement potentials. The longer an idea is exposed to new stimuli, the greater the potential for ideas to hybridize and evolve indefinitely toward problem resolution. An idea that is starved of new stimuli has a much lower potential to grow and evolve into something innovative. Figure 4 illustrates successive waves of hybridization through ideation and the dynamic of continual evolution of ideas, and ultimately the unlimited potential of ideas through constant exposure to new ideas.

Highly interactive educational environments are a necessity for collaborative creative practice: they provide the essential ideational fuel that leads to innovation and invention.

Outcomes Known to Outcomes Unknown, and Extrinsic to Intrinsic Motivation

In *Creative Development: Transforming Education through Design Thinking, Innovation, and Invention* (Kelly, 2016), I describe the dynamics that affect ideational growth and development. In consumption-intense educational discourses, the generation of ideas is stunted due to the phenomenon of early closure or right-answer syndrome. Learners are socialized into educational environments where the outcomes of learning are known and assessment becomes an exercise in restating the required outcomes to meet curricular requirements. There is no incentive for experimentation in this context, because learners spend a lot of time and energy predicting, remembering, and sourcing the right answers that signify educational success in an educational context focused solely on knowledge acquisition. Students in this context develop risk-averse dispositions, where any kind of experimentation, or veering from the required outcomes, could potentially result in punitive assessment. An educational culture of collaborative creativity includes necessary knowledge acquisition, but goes well beyond to encompass equipping learners and educators with a creative disposition and its corresponding tactics and strategies. The transformative dynamic of *outcomes known to outcomes unknown* in this educational context depends on generative interactivity to fuel ideation and prototype development, leading to problem refinement and resolution. Prototyping by its very nature is experimentation. It is an opportunity to test out a problem resolution in the currency of the discipline where this takes place. Socializing learners to become risk averse runs counter to being collaboratively creative. Learners must come to understand that experimentation is essential for creative outcomes, and that experimentation ultimately yields innovative rewards. This is a very large leap for learners transitioning to a culture of collaborative creativity, and the transition is often fraught with anxiety and mistrust at first. This unease dissipates once learners engage in the collaborative design process, which they discover is a pathway to collective innovation in response to a real-world problem for a real-world audience, an achievement with far deeper and broader implications than a letter grade.

Measurement to Development, Assets to Access, and Competitive to Collaborative

The key transformative dynamic of *measurement to development* involves changing the way learners are assessed. Traditional educational discourses constantly measure success through formal tests and outcomes designed to ensure learners are meeting system standards. Assessment is typically steeped in a culture of measuring knowledge acquisition. This results in a competitive culture and a hierarchical perception of success as a learner. A hypercompetitive culture can provoke high anxiety in learners from being judged by educators and being publicly compared to peers. I don't know many people who like to be publicly exposed as less successful than others, or who like constant reminders that they are not successful. In addition, for educators, it is very hard to gain the full trust of a student if the student perceives the educator to be constantly judging them, especially if a student is struggling to succeed within a machine bureaucracy organizational structure. This dynamic can create emotional distance between the learner and the educator, and between the learner and the institution or organization, resulting in dissociation (Kelly, 2012, 2016). Competition with fellow learners within a vertical assessment hierarchy can potentially lead to mistrust and the commodification of knowledge, because learners in this system may perceive exchanging ideas with fellow competitors as giving away an advantage when all are competing for the highest recognition. This precludes the free flow of ideas and stunts the development of the foundational attributes of a collaborative culture. Trust is very limited and the necessary interactivity to enable the proliferation of ideas for creative production gives way to high valuation of the possession of knowledge.

Benammar et al. (2014) discuss the transformative dynamic of *assets to access*, which speaks to the need to evolve to a different sensibility. "In education, it means shifting from memorizing facts to knowing where to find information. The new skill is searching for and evaluating information" ("THNK Paradigm Shifts Model," para. 3, point 3). Discipline knowledge is easily accessible using the connectivity of the Internet through any number of search engines. Emphasis has shifted from a disproportionate focus on the memorization of discipline content to the development of a capacity to access rapidly expanding discipline databases.

Recently, I was invited to speak at a postsecondary business school on the topic of creativity in teaching and learning. During my visit, I was invited to sit in on faculty workshops and provide feedback. One of the more interesting sessions was devoted to assessment. Cheating on examinations was discussed. I was amazed at the lengths students would go to use technology to cheat on exams. In the ensuing breakout groups, this question came up: Why are we making exams that ask for answers you can google? The question undermined the whole premise of traditional assessment, with its hyper-focus on knowledge accumulation and retention. Later, a working group within the faculty reported on a code of ethics it had produced for examinations for both instructors and students. On hearing the code of ethics, my feedback was quite direct. I stated that I could have been a prison warden talking to my staff and inmates with the same code of ethics. There is something fundamentally wrong here, and with any similar educational environment, where students have dissociated from the institution and its processes so much that they are compelled to engage in cheating. One thing has to be understood: the educators were all very caring people with a vested interest in their students and a genuine desire for all students to succeed. The organizational structure of the machine bureaucracy, with its focus on standardization and corresponding assessment regimens to ensure standards were being met, inadvertently placed instructors and learners in an oppositional, and sometimes adversarial, relationship characterized by complete mistrust on either side.

Push to Pull: Authoritative to Empowering, Top-Down to Emergent Design, and Pedagogy to Sociogogy

The final cluster of transformative dynamics encompasses *push to pull* (Hagel & Brown, 2005; Hagel, Brown, & Davison, 2010), *authoritative to empowering, top-down to emergent design* (Benammar et al., 2014), and *pedagogy to sociogogy* (Saveri & Chwierut, 2011). Collectively, they point to a transition to an educational culture where the needs of learner-initiated innovation and invention, including variability in those needs, necessitate rapid adaptability and recruitment of pertinent resources. The idea of *push* in *push to pull* references a very typical orientation to mandated curricula described by Hagel and Brown (2005): "In education, we design standard curricula to expose students to codified information in a predetermined sequence of experiences" (p. 3). There is very little room in this context for student-initiated collaborative creative production, because the raison d'être for the whole system is standardization. Therefore, the content of learning is largely predetermined, along with instructional design and corresponding assessment regimens. The push-to-pull transformative dynamic speaks to a sensibility that allows us to not only adapt, but to thrive, in a rapidly changing world. Hagel and Brown add, "Rather than 'push,' this new approach focuses on 'pull'—creating platforms that help people to mobilize appropriate resources when the need arises" (p. 4). They further elaborate:

> Push models treat people as passive consumers (even when they are producers like workers on an assembly line) whose needs can be anticipated and shaped by centralized decision makers. Pull models treat people as networked creators (even when they are customers purchasing goods and services) who are uniquely positioned to transform uncertainty from a problem into an opportunity. Pull models are ultimately designed to accelerate capability building by participants, helping them to learn as well as innovate, by pursuing trajectories of learning that are tailored to their specific needs. (p. 4)

The *authoritative to empowering* and *top-down to emergent design* dynamics further add to this need to accelerate the capability building of learners. They go beyond acquisition of knowledge to building educational environments that enable learner-initiated innovation. One could argue that having vast quantities of knowledge in a discipline is on its own empowering, allowing one to have a deep understanding of that discipline. However, a passive culture of compliance and cooperation is not empowering. True empowerment in education equips learners with the tactics, strategies, empathy, and interactive skills and creative capacity to invent and innovate for the benefit of others in a highly interconnected environment that is changing rapidly. This implies that educational design must accommodate a transfer of ownership for learning and creative-production initiation to learners. This is a very challenging prospect for educators who have only known traditional educational discourses, where educator control is paramount. The tactics and strategies for the innovation and invention required to both adapt to rapid change, and to initiate rapid change, require learner ownership, and not sole reliance on top-down, authoritative, external prompts and routines. Valuing intrinsic motivation is essential in a learner-empowered environment of collaborative, emergent design.

The *pedagogy to sociogogy* transformative dynamic adds another dimension to this shift of how we approach fundamental change toward collaborative creativity in the design of educational practice. The etymology of the word *pedagogy* implies that children are led, and in some contexts connotes a sense of paternalism. This resonates with the authoritative, top-down, push orientations that were previously discussed. The word *pedagogy* is also commonly used in the context of describing approaches to teaching. Saveri and Chwierut (2011) coined the term *sociogogy* to describe the new sensibility required to adapt to the realities of rapid sociocultural, technological, and economic change, and rapidly developing connectivity. They explain the context and concept of the term *sociogogy*:

> The diffusion of Internet connectivity, mobile devices, and participatory media is disrupting this long tradition. The connected, open, and social media context is creating a new context for cultivating relationships among learners and teachers. Like the Internet itself, the structure of learning relationships is flattening, becoming more peer-based and networked than hierarchical, expert dependent, and "command and control" driven. Educator-learner relationships are becoming more co-creative and self-initiated by individual learners. Many have referred to this learning relationship shift as a move from the "sage on the stage" to "guide on the side," but in fact the transformation is more fundamental. Indeed the experimentation with networked, co-creative, peer-based relationships among learners suggests a shift from "pedagogy" to "sociogogy"—in which teachers and students are learning "companions" (from the Latin *socius*) leading one another. This shift entails a whole new framework for learning and co-creating knowledge. (p. 19)

This framework is characterized by a high degree of interactivity along with a rapid recruitment of pertinent resources, physical and virtual, to meet learning and creative production needs. It is also characterized by a flattened organizational structure that is more distributed and more lateral, which enables a free flow of resource recruitment conducive to agile adaptation to learner needs. Since they coined this term in a piece entitled "The Future of Learning Agents and Disruptive Innovation" for the Institute for the Future, change has been so rapid that the impetus for designing education around transformative dynamics has taken on greater importance. The development of new vocabulary such as *sociogogy* to describe forward adaptive design and innovation reflects the need to be flexible enough to embrace change as opportunity, not as threat. Coauthor Andrea Saveri expands on the concept of sociogogy in the fourth Collaborating to Create feature in this book.

The implications of the visualization, design, and implementation of the comprehensive list of transformative dynamics (Figure 2) is quite daunting for mainstream educators, whose only frame of reference is a standardized organizational and pedagogical sensibility. This creates an incredible inertia, making these systems almost impervious to fundamental reframing and reconceptualization. The prospect of disrupted routine and assumptions often provokes fear and anxiety. Many would view fundamental change to educational structure in response to the transformative dynamics as educational mayhem, because it lacks the cohesive structure and rules so familiar in a machine bureaucracy orientation. As previously discussed, adhocratic organizational structures actually have more complex structure, designed around creative production, not absence of structure.

A question that commonly arises when examining the prospect of transitioning toward a culture of collaborative creativity is: What happens to the central pillars of knowledge acquisition and corresponding assessments that are the indicators of success in a system built around standardization? How does one ensure that discipline-competency acquisition remains central to education? There is sometimes a false dichotomous perception that discipline knowledge suffers if you expand educational practice to focus on creative development. Educators who are resistant to change, or who are risk averse, often respond with this classic dichotomous argument. I can remember, as a graduate student in education, British philosopher David Best, one of my professors, calling this type of assumption "the disease of the dichotomous mind," meaning that if something is X then it cannot be Y, and vice versa. Discipline-competency acquisition and creative development are not mutually exclusive educational concepts. It is not a zero-sum game, where focus on one takes away from the other. Discipline-competency development, gaining more and more knowledge in any field, is an essential developmental strand to enable creative development. It is one of several developmental strands that comprehensively contribute to an increase in creative capacity and ultimately creative development.

Chapter 3, "A Framework for Collaborative Creativity in Educational Practice," explores an ecological conceptual framework built on the interrelatedness of educational developmental strands that inform comprehensive creative development in a culture of collaborative creativity. It moves the conversation on educational transformation away from traditional models, which have disproportionate emphasis on knowledge acquisition and its accompanying measurement, toward a model based on collaborative creativity conducive to creative development. Collaborative creativity embeds learners in meaningful contexts for discipline-competency acquisition, critical thinking, and other developmental strands, as the educational discourse moves from *consume* to *create*, from *passive* to *interactive*, and from *authoritative* to *empowered*. The transformative dynamics that lead to collaborative creativity provide learners with a much bigger toolkit, grounded in adapting to perpetual change and creating positive change for the benefit of others.

COLLABORATING TO CREATE 3

Karim Benammar on Paradigm Shifts and the Need for Reframing

EDITED BY ROBERT KELLY

Karim Benammar, PhD, is an independent philosopher specializing in transformative thinking. He gives lectures and workshops for companies and organizations. He is the author of *Abundance* and *Reframing/The Art of Thinking Differently*, as well as several online courses (www.karimbenammar.com).

Reframing: The Art of Thinking Differently

My current focus in my lectures and workshops is on Reframing—spelled with a capital *R* because it is a particular process. We can reframe our current perspective on three levels: the level of the individual, where it is often related to psychological patterns and scripts; the level of an organization, where we rethink business models and entrenched organizational models; and, finally, the societal level, where we can see large societal changes that we call paradigm shifts.

I am interested in two fundamental questions, which I consider to be deeply philosophical. First, why do we do the things that we do? And second, could we do things radically differently? Think of all the structures in our lives: our economic production-consumption system, our taxation systems, our education system, the way we organize leisure. These structures and frames are not "natural." They have evolved historically to become the dominant structures of our time. Why are they like that?

Which brings us to the companion question: Is there a way of doing things radically differently? What would it take? The world is constantly changing. Things change because of innovations and technology, because culture evolves, because of globalization. On a personal level, things change because we all get older and go through different stages in our lives. Individually and communally, we develop a frame, a structure, or a paradigm that works for our current reality, and initially it works pretty well. Then the reality changes, and the structure no longer works so well because it does not fit the evolving reality anymore. At some point, it starts to rub. When it starts rubbing a lot, it can become very painful. Structures are pretty rigid: they cannot evolve gradually. This creates a desire to find a new approach by changing that structure. You might as well change it in one fell swoop and make a big change, and you might as well make it future-proof, so that you can evolve into it.

A classic example is the radical changes the music industry had to undergo when music could be stored as digital data: successive shifts from records to compact discs to digital purchases to streaming. Similar disruptions are occurring in our working lives, with fewer fixed contracts and more freelance work and the gig economy. We are all living 10 or 20 years longer on average, so our pension systems have to change. The same thing is true of companies: Will there still be demand for a company's product in the future? What would be a radically new way to provide that product or service?

I have codified Reframing as a five-step process. The first two steps are related to our first question: Why is the world the way it is? We start by choosing a core belief or current situation. Then we ask: What are the assumptions underlying our way of doing things? For example: Why do we believe that eating fatty food is unhealthy? Why do we select educational cohorts based on age? Why are women paid less than men in our society? The assumptions underlying our thinking and actions are often unexamined, and therefore invisible. By mapping these assumptions and choosing the most important ones, we get a clear sense of our current structure. Then we need to find a way to let go of these assumptions and construct a new frame based on radically different assumptions.

How do we push ourselves out of these entrenched frames? The trick is to push our thinking in a direction it does not want to go. In the third step of Reframing, we force ourselves to turn our underlying assumptions into their extreme opposites. First, we construct grammatical opposites. This immediately leads to resistance, because you are saying the opposite of what you just thought. This resistance is a good sign. Instead of fighting it, go with the resistance, and make it stronger by turning the opposite into an extreme version. A classic example is when people analyze why they are too busy at work, which is often tied to an underlying assumption that makes them say yes to requests too often. The grammatical opposite is that they say no too often, or that they rarely say yes. Making it extreme, we get "I never say yes," or "whatever the request, the answer is no." This is a serious shock to the belief system of someone who usually says yes, but it also shifts them to a new perspective on their behaviour, into a new frame. People laugh a lot at this stage, because new frames often seem ridiculous at first. Soon, though, we realize that we know a lot of successful people who usually turn down requests, and that saying yes too much is actually a ridiculous—and not very effective—way of working. It doesn't mean that you're going to shift a full 180 degrees in the hour that the exercise takes. But you will no longer be certain that your initial assumptions are correct. Your mind is willing to play a game, and to think of a completely different world, even if your emotions resist that.

Reframing a belief or situation leads to new ways of thinking, and we want this to translate into new ways of acting. In the fourth step of Reframing, you envision a future scenario in which all your assumptions have turned into their extreme opposites. In the fifth step, you focus on one change that you can turn into a simple experiment. Design a no-cost or low-cost way to try a radically new approach, in order to test whether it is better than your old one. Take a small risk, without risking everything. The promise is that things might improve dramatically. This last step is effective, because the combination of low risk and potentially high reward is hard to resist. One just has to be open to it.

Paradigm Shifts and Their Implications for Educational Change

When Reframing happens on a large, societal scale, and is caused by waves of culture or technology rather than by a decision to examine one's beliefs, I call this a "paradigm shift." The notion comes from philosopher Thomas Kuhn's seminal work *The Structure of Scientific Revolutions*. Before Kuhn, the accepted narrative was that science, and our understanding of the world, improved gradually. As a historian of science, Kuhn argued that this process was not gradual, but happened in fits and starts. Kuhn describes what he calls a paradigm, a way of looking at the world. A paradigm can be dominant for centuries, but, at a certain point, experimental data does not fit the old paradigm anymore, which leads some scientists to rethink the dominant model. Some propose a radically new approach, which is fiercely resisted by the "old guard." It really has to be a revolution.

Kuhn gives two large-scale examples of paradigm shifts. The first example is the shift from a geocentric view of the solar system, with Earth at the centre, to a heliocentric view, with the sun at the centre. The second example is the revolution of quantum mechanics, when scientists started to postulate that very, very small things behave according to different laws than those described by Newtonian physics. But there are many other examples of paradigm shifts, in which our model is completely upended and a new way of understanding the world takes its place. The resistance to the new approach also shows how deeply ingrained our beliefs tend to become. There is a disturbing historical example in breast cancer treatment. For a long time, the approach to mastectomies was that the more tissue you took away, the better the chance of survival. So, top surgeons developed "radical surgery." Then research proved that, in fact, radical surgery does not improve survival chances, because it does not address the way cancer actually spreads. But radical surgery continued for another decade, despite compelling, contradictory evidence. It was the way surgeons were trained, and it was the way surgeons were thinking.

As part of our curriculum design at the THNK School of Creative Leadership, we focused on some key paradigm shifts that we believe are taking place today. In my workshops, I ask people whether they recognize these shifts in their specific field, and what consequences this has for their way of thinking and acting. Do they need to reframe their approach to be successful in the new paradigm? Here are three paradigm shifts with implications about how we can transition to completely new ways of thinking about educational practice.

The paradigm shift from *push* to *pull* is a radical change in our approach to many situations: we tend to push structures onto people. We don't ask students what they want, we don't ask employees what they want, we don't ask citizens what they want. Instead, we tell them what will happen. Teachers tell students, doctors tell patients, managers tell employees, civil servants tell citizens, and so on. Mainstream education is an instructive example of a push system. The curriculum is pushed at students who are told what they need to know in each field. The assumption is that students are not in a position to know what is good for them—this requires the judgement of professionals. The speed of learning is also fixed, even though a curriculum designed for the average student disempowers both those who cannot keep up and those who are being held back because they are not sufficiently challenged. Most of our schools are still nothing more than a production line where students are pushed through an educational program that is predefined, evaluated through exams, and rewarded with a degree.

Pull education, by contrast, is based on the needs of learners as articulated by the individual student. Students need to have a clear idea of where they want to go, and ask for the learning programs, educational materials, and teacher support they need for their progress. An online platform can be of great value in matching learning needs with teaching offerings. Many people object that students cannot formulate their learning needs, because they don't know enough about what there is to learn. But young people already use this strategy in a different area. Think about how young people learn to develop romantic relationships: once the need presents itself, they actively search for information, talk to peers, and ask advice from those they trust. They learn through experiment, trial, and error. While some pull models of education are clear, it is incredibly difficult to make the shift in practice. The typical physical infrastructure of schools, including buildings, classrooms, and cohorts, is only adequate for a push model.

A related paradigm shift goes from *consume* to *create*, from passive consumer to active creator. Education is for the most part, despite some outstanding exceptions, based on a unidirectional, authoritative, and disempowering structure, in which the student is often totally passive. Students are usually not involved in structuring their education, in co-authoring educational textbooks, or in co-designing a curriculum. Making a shift to a paradigm of student co-creation could lead to substantial student ownership of their learning and a much greater potential for student innovation.

A third paradigm shift is from *assets* to *access*, the shift from owning goods to using and sharing goods. You replace having an asset with access to a service. The shift from assets to access is not limited to material goods. It is also happening on an educational level. Most of mainstream education is based on memorizing facts: you have to stockpile learned facts in your head, which then become your knowledge assets. But, today, all you need to know is where to find the information: you need access to relevant databases or online repositories. The skills required in education are undergoing a dramatic shift from memorizing and learning to knowing how to navigate your way around information, and to use that information as knowledge.

Thinking in terms of paradigm shifts allows us to design possibilities for radically new collaborative structures of education, while also recognizing the large structural impediments to change. I openly encourage educational experimentation: try radically new things in a controlled setting, and try many different things. Change will happen through a multitude of small revolutions.

Andrea Saveri on Shifting from Pedagogy to Sociogogy

EDITED BY ROBERT KELLY

Andrea Saveri heads up Saveri Consulting, where her work with education clients has focused on making the future actionable through research-based foresight, highly creative engagement experiences, and visual maps and artifacts. Andrea is skilled at conducting quantitative and qualitative research, applying futures methodologies, and designing breakthrough collaboration experiences. She has creatively collaborated with major research universities, community colleges, and K to 12 schools to develop strategies and implement action for 21st century education. She spent 21 years at the Institute for the Future in Palo Alto, California, leading global research and forecasting projects in education, health, and the workplace. She is a graduate of Harvard University (BA, Hispanic studies) and of the University of California, Berkeley (MA, Latin American studies).

The Beginnings of Sociogogy

The term *sociogogy* was coined by my colleague Matt Chwierut and me while we were collaborating on a project for the KnowledgeWorks Foundation (an educational nonprofit organization) more than a decade ago. We were exploring how emerging networked media could shape the future context of education and enable new roles to support teaching and learning. Back then, we were in the early days of social media and thinking about open education. So, we started to ask ourselves: What could teaching and learning look like in a world with robust social networking and media platforms? We looked at the origins of the term *pedagogy*, which comes from the Greek practice of assigning a slave—literally a leader (*agagos* in Greek) of children—to walk boys to school, from tutor to tutor, and generally supervise them as they prepared for life in Greek society. This hierarchical teacher-student relationship, of an adult leading a child through a course of sequential study, had persisted in a basic form over the years. We wondered what teaching and learning might look like if social media and networking could break down that hierarchical teacher-student relationship and the linear, sequential process of going from one subject to the next. We thought about what we would call a learning system that leveraged a more peer-to-peer, many-to-many, social-network-based format and framework. We played around with terms and came up with the idea of "social pedagogy"—in other words, the social group as the leader of learning, not a single supervisor or teacher. We imagined the possibility of these nascent social networking and social media technologies enabling a type of teaching and learning universe that is driven by real social interaction—by peer-to-peer, many-to-many kinds of rich social engagement. I think that was the big idea behind sociogogy. I think we still need to discover and develop the kinds of organizational structures and infrastructure that can really support the richness of this kind of peer-to-peer education.

The concept of sociogogy highlights the social interactions and social relationships that are a core part of learning. And this doesn't have to mean social relationships that are enabled by technology, but any kind of group-driven or group-situated learning that leverages social relationships. Thinking about it today, the discipline of sociology reminds us of the importance of the social in human interactions that stimulate discovery and discussion, debate, and reflection. These are all important aspects of cognitive and metacognitive growth. So, if we take sociogogy and the richness that it suggests, then how do we create a whole system and infrastructure that can support a flourishing of the social and human relationships in learning?

The Importance of Human Development

Today, focusing on supporting human development and healthy social relationships as a foundation for learning is more important than ever. Advances in digital automation of work tasks and augmentation of human cognition are redefining how humans contribute in the workplace. Smart devices and AI are getting smarter and doing more complex cognitive tasks. They're doing work tasks that make up a lot of middle-class jobs and knowledge work. We have to learn how to develop more productive and meaningful partnerships with technology, and how to constantly adapt to a changing world of work. In education, the societal narrative has to shift from knowledge acquisition to a focus on increasing creative capacity, individual agency, and productive partnerships with technologies that augment what we as humans can uniquely do. As technologies do more cognitive tasks at work, we need to focus on the relational and uniquely human aspects of work that are so important, like caring for people and stimulating their creativity, building creative climates and partnerships, and using our intuition, emotions, and humour to build relationships and come up with new ideas. We have to do the things that AI can't do—yet. Parents, colleges, and the whole educational ecosystem have to buy into this for it to happen. And this isn't just a shift to student-centred education, but a shift to truly human-centred education. We have to invest in developing a young person's social and emotional core, and sense of self, of who they are as a human person. You can't develop creative capacity without that. And students won't be able to navigate a changing world without it.

Adapting to a Changing World

Today's students are moving into a world that will involve massive displacement and transformation of work. They're going to have to deal with incredible volatility and change. We often hear the saying in education, "We're trying to educate students for jobs that don't exist yet with technologies that aren't developed yet." So what do you do? You give students a foundation that will set them up to be adaptive, resilient, and self-guiding, and this relies on a strong sense of self, core human-relationship building, and emotion-regulation skills.

You can't have sociogogy unless you have capable individuals who can relate with other people, get into disagreement, get into situations of discomfort, and build bridges across difference. This includes failing, and working with difficult situations. These are developmental capacities, and they're not at all at the centre of mainstream educational practice. Unless we address that, we won't develop creative capacity, and we won't build an education system around sociogogy and the unique qualities of being human, which is how to be in relationship with other people.

3

A Framework for Collaborative Creativity in Educational Practice

Educational Socialization: What Has Informed our Understanding of What Education Is?

I can recall the first day of a fall semester, teaching a fourth-year university painting class of 16 students in a bachelor of fine arts program. All of them had shown up to the first class with a number of rectangular, flat, white canvases to paint on, even though it wasn't indicated on the course outline. I guess to anyone without art training or an art background that would make sense, because one would assume from our socialization, and by what we usually put on our living room walls, as well as pictures of famous paintings like the *Mona Lisa*, that a painting is flat and rectangular. It is what we have come to know and accept about what a painting is. Anyone with any art training at all would know that this isn't the limit of what painting is, in either historical or contemporary practice. Artists over time have explored any number of irregular painted surfaces, shapes, contexts, and configurations. Of course, historically, there is a critical mass of flat-surfaced, rectangular formats, but this critical mass does not define the limit of possibilities for painting. I confronted the students about their assumption that paintings had to be rectangular and flat. I also asked if all of their ideas were rectangular and flat. The students were exhibiting what Arthur Koestler (1964) describes, in one of my favourite quotes, as the "anaesthesia of conditioning." We become socialized into complacency, thinking a certain context is the way things are always done, precluding any number of innovative potentials for exploration, growth, and development. The students had acquiesced to a cultural convention without question. They had inadvertently limited themselves from exploring an unlimited number of creative outcomes because of the anaesthesia of conditioning.

We can apply Koestler's lens to the critical mass of educators and educational administrators who are imbued with educational practice built around standardization within machine bureaucracy organizational structures that emphasize knowledge acquisition and measurement. Achievement is viewed through measurable standards that become critical grade-point averages for postsecondary admission and beyond. This has become what most consider traditional education. This is the rectangular, flat, white canvas that conditioning has made us understand as "education." Mintzberg (1989), in his early work on the structure of organizations, confronted conditioning when he had difficulty describing organizational structures for innovation to a publisher. He made this reflection: "To many people—especially conventional consultants and government people ... machine bureaucracy is not just one possible form of structure, it *is* structure. It is not the one best way. It is the only way" (p. 197). This applies today to the tremendous inertia that impedes fundamental educational change. Chapter 2 describes how the transformative dynamics at play in a sea of constant, rapid change are limited in their transformational potentials because of the inertia of an entrenched understanding of what education is. This widespread flat-rectangular-canvas view of education is so deep-rooted that, in order to begin the transition to an educational culture of collaborative creativity, we must engage in resocialization or reframing. This involves introspection about how one has acquired the perceptions one holds, while raising awareness of views or potentials that may at first appear counterintuitive in the context of previously held views. The point in the transitional process where the transformative dynamics begin to generate change causes immense anxiety for many, usually associated with not being able to visualize where the change is headed. The anxiety is easy to understand: many have no direct experience of collaborative creative practice in their formal education or personal experience. Actual engagement in collaborative creative practice provides a path forward to the discovery of new dispositions and ways of being in the world, as one sees firsthand the vast educational potentials of this way of being. Chapter 5, "Giant Lobsters, Whales, and Elephants: A Case Study in Developing an Educational Culture of Collaborative Creativity," examines the development of, and transition to, collaborative culture in an educational context and the resocialization necessary to make this transition.

Figure 5 represents an estimation of a typical learner's journey through an education system based on examination of mandated curricula, course outlines, and long-range plans of educators from early childhood to postsecondary levels. This is not empirical data, but rather a compilation

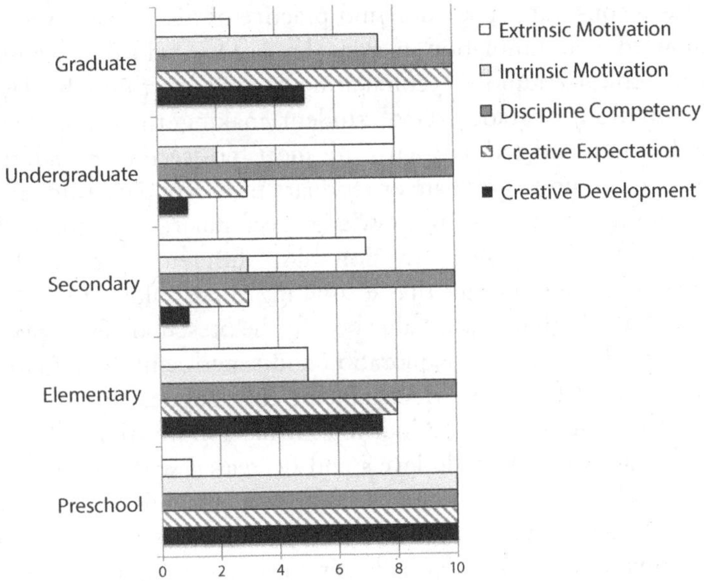

FIGURE 5. Observations of longitudinal creative development and expectation

of observations from a variety of commentators, including graduate students in education, practising educators in the field, postsecondary faculty in education and science, and my own examination of provincial K to 12 curricula across disciplines. It is an attempt show how we come to be socialized in formal education and come to develop a perception of what education is. The notion of resocialization or reframing for the purpose of initiating and adapting to educational change begins with this process, because we have to establish what experiences have gone into our educational journey.

The *extrinsic* and *intrinsic motivation* values in Figure 5 represent an attempt (an admittedly difficult task) to estimate time spent as a learner in either orientation. The motivation values connect to the concept of ownership: of whether learning is driven by the teacher or system, or by the learner. The *discipline competency* value estimates the expectation and practice of acquiring knowledge across disciplines. The *creative expectation* value estimates the expectation that a learner has the capacity to create innovative responses and initiatives. The *creative development* value estimates the time spent by a learner in actual creative practice, contributing to growing creative development and increasing creative capacity.

As the estimations in Figure 5 illustrate, commentators gave discipline competency the maximum 10 value at each level. They generally felt that there was a constant expectation and practice of discipline competency and knowledge accumulation at every level. This held true whether it was a preschooler rapidly accumulating knowledge through play and experimentation; a grade school student making their way through standardized, mandated curricula to meet postsecondary admission standards; or an undergraduate or graduate postsecondary student, who takes on high expectations of knowledge accumulation. Commentators gave extrinsic and intrinsic motivation values different scores at different levels, while acknowledging that estimating these values was difficult. They felt that a high intrinsic value best fit the preschool level, given the general high disposition of exploration and experimentation. Gardner's (1980) notion of U-shaped development corroborates this view. They felt that, through the K to 12 journey, intrinsic motivation values were highest at the younger grade levels and decreased with progression to secondary school, where discipline-competency acquisition, standardized achievement tests, and postsecondary admissions standards placed more emphasis on knowledge acquisition and measurement, and less emphasis on student-initiated innovation and invention. Commentators observed that the inverse was true for extrinsic motivation values: these values grow with progression through secondary school and into undergraduate postsecondary education, as students become bombarded with masses of discipline content from experts in the field. At the graduate level, commentators reversed the values of extrinsic and intrinsic motivation, compared to the undergraduate level, because students become engaged in focus areas where they have a high level of personal interest and knowledge in a discipline area. As emerging researchers, graduate students are typically expected to contribute new kernels of knowledge to their chosen discipline or field. Commentators felt that creative expectation generally tracks the value of intrinsic motivation.

Graduate work involves an expectation of innovation or creative outcome, whether learners have a high creative capacity or not. We have all heard at one time or another an educator asking learners to "be creative" or "use your imaginations" or "think outside the box." Without consistent developmental creative practice from early childhood to postsecondary levels, it is unfair to make the assumption that learners at any particular level have a commensurate creative capacity. Interestingly, after several years of education with a hyper-focus on knowledge acquisition and measurement, and considerably less focus on creative development, graduate students are all of sudden expected to create original research. Adam Royalty, formerly of Stanford's d.school K12 lab, pointedly asks why we have to wait until someone is in their early twenties before we can trust them to create something original (as cited in Kelly, 2012). A central educational emphasis on continual creative development and increasing creative capacity would lead to an empowered educational culture, with exponentially greater innovation and invention potentials at all levels, which would address the disparity that now exists in graduate studies between high creative expectation and little preparation through creative growth and development.

In education, we get good at what we practise. If we practise the tactics and strategies of knowledge acquisition, retention, and measurement, we get good at that. The socialized patterns associated with this learning culture become ingrained in the behavioural patterns of the learner. If that is the vast majority of our educational experience, we come to know this as what education is.

Collaborative Creativity: The Catalytic Foundation for Creative Development

An educational culture of collaborative creativity goes well beyond these commonly held socialized perceptions of what education is. It embraces a different emphasis, and a different ecosystem of the interrelated developmental strands necessary for systematic creative development of the learner, than traditional educational practice. Transitioning to an educational culture of collaborative creativity requires a tangible vision or framework that informs educational practice, and that comes from this different approach. In Kelly (2012), I presented a preliminary prototype of a framework describing the interrelationships of developmental strands that collectively contribute to growth in the creative capacity and creative development of the learner. In that preliminary framework, creative development was described as the growth from the natural human disposition of intuitive/adaptive creativity to the development of capacities to engage in increasingly complex, sustained creative practice characterized by original research and production that has increasing sociocultural relevance and importance. Eight interrelated developmental strands contributed to a learner's creative developmental growth, starting with collaborative development, and including self-instigative development, research/investigative development, generative (ideation) development, experimentational (prototyping) development, discipline complexity, critical thinking, and creative sustain development. At the time, I was a visiting scholar at a Canadian postsecondary institution. One of my graduate students in education approached me with the idea that collaborative development was central to enabling the other developmental strands, and therefore should have greater emphasis. I had been presenting the strands as more or less equal or balanced. She argued that collaboration was catalytic in maximizing the interactivity that would amplify the other developmental strands. Her point was well taken, influencing the further development of this prototype framework.

The primary educational lab for developing this framework prototype and its ensuing iterations is a series of graduate programs in education that I designed and teach that are focused on creative development, design thinking for innovation, and collaborative creativity at the Werklund School of Education at my home institution. The work in this lab has been augmented with further prototyping experiments at other institutions at both the undergraduate and graduate levels. Getting constructive comments from that graduate student, and other program and class participants, was very much part of the feedback loop necessary in the design process to advance this concept and to refine successive prototypes toward refinement and resolution. This conceptual framework for creative development has gone through several iterations of prototyping since its inception in 2012. Little did I know that my graduate student's feedback in 2012 would inspire prototype change and refinement, and end up as an entire book devoted to collaborative creativity.

Figure 6 represents the most recent version of this framework, with nine interrelated developmental strands, which one could still consider a prototype because it is still evolving in response to continuous research and against a backdrop of constant change. Regardless, it is a conceptual framework from which to visualize and inform educational practice within a culture of collaborative creativity. The developmental strands in Figure 6 are not meant to be viewed as linear, but rather as concurrent, interrelated developmental components that ebb and flow relative to each other depending on the capacity of a learner within a longitudinal, creative initiative. Figure 6 represents an educational/ecological perspective on the interrelatedness of developmental strands necessary to enable a culture of collaborative creativity across the discipline spectrum. The strands also lend themselves to learning-experience design and assessment design for creative development. This shifts the emphasis from educational cultures focused disproportionately on discipline content acquisition and commensurate assessment regimens to a pedagogical and sociogogical discourse enabling increasingly complex collaborative, creative production by both educator and learner. It is important to note that discipline knowledge acquisition is an essential component in this framework. As stated earlier, creative production is built around growing discipline knowledge and understanding, along with other essential developmental components. However, in the context of this creative development framework, discipline-competency acquisition serves creative production in concert with accompanying developmental strands, as opposed to being the primary rationale for educational practice. This represents perhaps the single most difficult conceptual transition for educators to make. The creative development framework is an attempt to explain how these concepts are not mutually exclusive or isolated, but rather complementary through their interrelatedness. They amplify knowledge acquisition by providing relevant knowledge-acquisition contexts through a primary focus on creative practice in a different educational ecosystem. This equips the learner (and educator) with the tactics, strategies, and disposition of design practice for creative production leading to invention and innovation. Compared to traditional knowledge-transfer-and-retention educational discourses, this ultimately gives the learner and educator a much larger and more effective toolkit to deal with the increasing complexities of rapid sociocultural, economic, and environmental change.

The difficulty of transitioning to a culture of collaborative creativity is best alleviated by firsthand educator experience in creative production that requires collaborative creativity. The creative development framework enables this practical application and experience, which fuels the transitional impetus into this new culture. Collaborative development, along with its sister developmental strand, communication, enhances the collective innovation potential of the other creative developmental strands and the whole creative development dynamic.

The Anatomy of Creative Development Through Collaborative Creativity

Figure 6 depicts the interrelatedness of the nine developmental strands that contribute to creative development. It also shows the direction of growth in creative capacity, starting with our natural human disposition of intuitive/adaptive creativity. This represents what Csikszentmihalyi (1996) characterizes as "small *c* creativity" or the adaptive creativity that human beings innately possess and deploy in everyday living. Figure 6 shows creative development growing upward, toward a deeper and broader capacity to engage in sustained creative practice in increasingly more complex problems requiring recurrent iterations of ideation and prototyping over time. Eventually, this leads to the development of original research and production engaging collaborative innovation networks. The creative-capacity growth bar on the right-hand side of

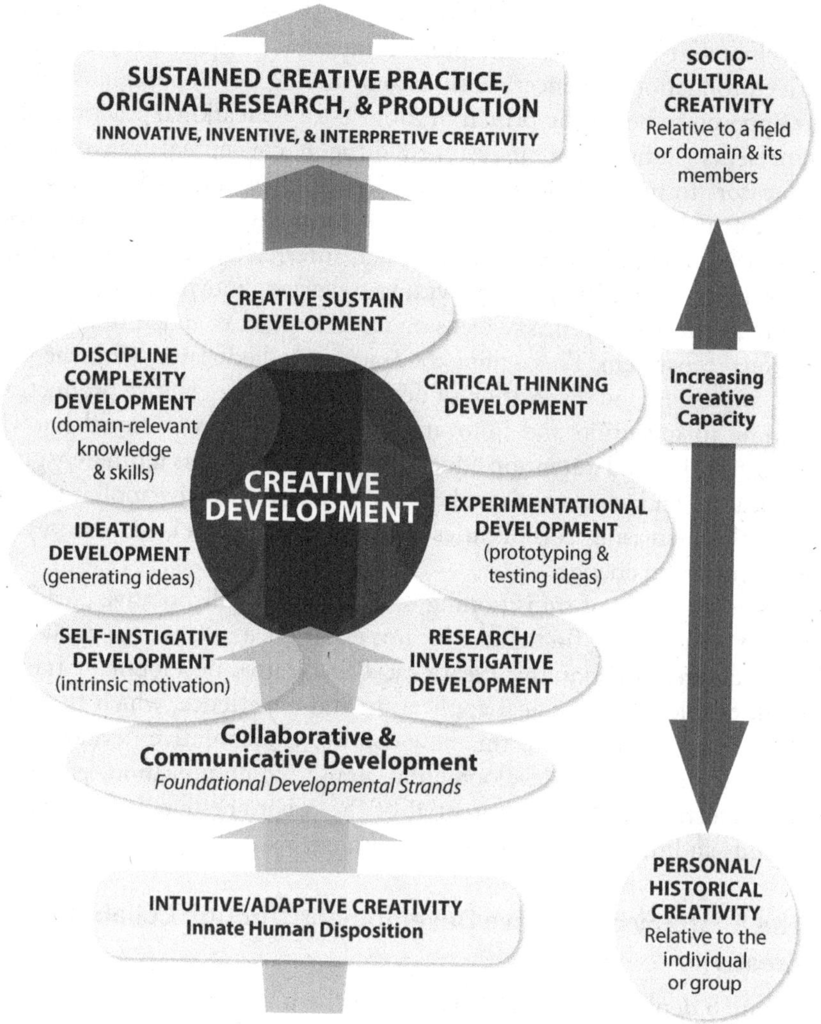

FIGURE 6. Creative development

Figure 6 shows a learner's growth in creative capacity throughout their educational journey. In the early formative stages of creative development, the originality of a learner's creative output is assessed through a personal/historical perspective, where a learner's work is compared to their previous output for degree of originality. As creative capacity increases, and creative output grows in complexity, the output eventually gains relevance to the field or domain in which it is occurring, and is judged for originality by members of that field through a sociocultural perspective (Sawyer, 2012).

This creative development framework was designed with educational cultural transition in mind. It aims to articulate, in an accessible way, the operationalizing of collaborative creativity in educational practice, and to inform learning-experience design and assessment design for creative development. Questions often arise in the field of creativity in education, such as: Can we teach creativity? Can we teach someone to be creative? How do we assess creativity? These questions are attempts to understand operationalizing creativity in educational practice. However, these questions are problematic in that they come from traditional educational discourses that emphasize knowledge transfer and retention. Creativity is a discipline largely located in the area of psychology. Runco's (2014) book *Creativity: Theories and Themes: Research, Development, and Practice* is testimony to this: it has a reference list that is 55 pages long, with citations largely from the psychology domain. In a traditional educational discourse, one could gather a tremendous amount of knowledge and learn a lot about creativity. As previously discussed, it is a misconception to assume that a high degree of discipline knowledge implies that one has high creative capacity. Creative development and growing creative capacity come only with engagement in increasingly complex iterations of creative practice over time, involving concurrent, interrelated developmental strands that are collectively necessary to grow the creative capacity of an individual or group. In this context, discipline-complexity development is one of many interrelated, essential components of creative development, not the sole focus of educational practice. A more appropriate question when it comes to operationalizing creativity in educational practice is: How do we create educational environments that are conducive to creative development? The creative development framework breaks creative development down into nine identifiable developmental strands that serve to bring both precision and scope to applying creativity in educational practice. Each developmental strand in concert with the others contributes to the creative growth of the learner.

Collaborative and communicative development are combined to form a foundational developmental strand in this framework. They amplify the other seven developmental strands optimizing innovation potential. Chapter 1 describes collaboration, in the context of collaborative creativity, as having the following attributes: the group exists for novel, adaptive, creative production; the diversity of group members is leveraged toward shared creative production; there is a shift from ego-centric to group-centric dispositions of group members; there is high interactivity among group members, with communication characterized by open-mindedness, empathy, flexibility, active and deep listening, respect, and honesty; and the potential creative outcomes of the collaborative group would be impossible, or highly unlikely, to achieve as an individual. The quality and nature of the communication among group members is critical to collaborative development, which explains the rationale for combining collaboration and communication into one foundational developmental strand. The nature of the communication among group members is also the most critical signifier of collaborative development.

Interactivity in the form of deep and active listening is central to collaborative development. There are numerous models available for deep or active listening in a collaborative environment. I have adapted a four-level model from Cohen (2014) as a means to analyze communication among members of a collaborative group as a signifier of growth in collaborative development.

Level 1 in this listening model involves physical or attentive listening. This is based primarily on physical cues like maintaining eye contact, leaning toward the speaker, and squarely facing the person that is speaking. When listening, one has to physically attend to the primary speaker. Sadly, in traditional, didactic educational discourses, this is quite often the level of listening development expected from the learner. In this context, the learner is perceived to be compliant and cooperative with a greater potential to retain the knowledge being transmitted. Whereas this might be the upper limit of listening development in traditional educational practice, it is the first of four communicative developmental levels for deep, active listening in a culture of collaborative creativity. Although it is the first step toward active and deep listening, when it is the upper limit of listening development, it is indicative of an educational environment that is largely passive.

Level 2 in developing active and deep listening is the interpretive level. This involves interactivity revolving around seeking clarification of what is being said through restatement, paraphrasing, and interpretation. This level demonstrates that the listener is actively trying to understand the speaker. This not only validates what the speaker is saying, but also helps the speaker clarify their own thoughts by hearing their thoughts spoken back to them.

Level 3, empathetic listening, is built around providing and growing empathy. This moves the interactivity of communication from a preliminary intellectual connection to one that encompasses understanding the emotional basis surrounding the communicator and their communication. It involves seeing the world the way others see it without judgement, and understanding the emotional disposition of the communicator. Empathetic listening is critical in developing trust among members of a collaborative group. Trust among collaborative group members gives everyone a feeling of a safe environment where they can feel free to put their ideas forward, or make mistakes, without being admonished or receiving any other kind of punitive response from group members. This is so essential in enabling the proliferation of ideas and experimentation central to creative practice. Ultimately, the creation of a safe environment for idea generation, growth, and development leads to a brave collaborative environment, where experimentation flourishes as risk aversion decreases. This is conducive to Level 4 listening that is highly generative.

Level 4 listening involves building on each other's thoughts. Cohen (2014) describes this as "when you listen beyond words and feelings. It is when you forge a connection with a person in such a deep way you become generative with your hearing—adding more, much more than what is being said" ("Level 4: Acting generatively," para. 1). This level of communication allows ideas to multiply freely and exponentially, without fear, in a communicative and collaborative environment that is truly group-centric, or eco-centric (Scharmer & Kaufer, 2013). The foundational nature of the combined collaborative and communicative developmental strands lies in its positive catalyzing influence on the other developmental strands essential for creative development.

Self-instigative development represents the transition from an extrinsic motivational orientation to a disposition of intrinsic motivation in educational practice. An intrinsically motivated learner or educator is driven by internal rewards, gaining personal satisfaction from their efforts to create or resolve a problem. Self-instigative development implies an intentional focus in learning-experience design built around learner-owned learning experiences that lead to learner-initiated innovation and invention. Amabile and Pratt (2016) point out that an intrinsically motivated disposition has a highly positive effect on increasing creative potential and output, building on Teresa Amabile's earlier pioneering work in the area of intrinsic motivation and creativity. Fischer, Malycha, and Schafmann (2019) corroborate this notion through an empirical study, stating that "an explicitly strong and significantly positive main effect is found between intrinsic motivation and creative/innovative performance" (p. 9).

In passive educational discourses focused on knowledge transfer and retention, extrinsic motivation predominates: the educator often provides the motivation to complete learning episodes in a standardized curriculum environment. Skillful educators go to extreme ends to make remote curricula relevant and interesting for learners. Student innovation is sometimes encouraged in this educational environment, but usually in the context of serving knowledge retention. Innovation can be expected, but most likely in response to a standardized preset where outcomes are already known, as opposed to student-initiated innovation and invention where exploration may lead to a place of outcomes unknown. In an educational culture of collaborative creativity, knowledge acquisition and retention serve creative production, echoing Amabile and Pratt's (2016) componential model of creativity, where domain-relevant knowledge and skills combine with creativity-relevant knowledge and skills, and task motivation, to create conditions conducive to creative practice. Educational design that deliberately transfers the ownership of innovation and invention to the learner over time is essential to developing a disposition of intrinsic motivation, which in turn is essential for enhanced sustained creative output from the learner. The foundational combination of collaborative and communicative development creates an educational environment of high interactivity. This interactivity is characterized by active and deep listening development toward empathetic and generative listening. Fischer et al. (2019) confirm that relational validation enhances intrinsic motivation and, ultimately, creative production.

Research/investigative development represents a developmental transition from a solely passive research disposition to an active, experiential, investigative disposition. Passive traditional research has its place and value, because the masses of literature-based research that are rapidly expanding and easily accessible serve the growth of domain-relevant knowledge and skills specific to any creative initiative. In a culture of collaborative creativity, the development of an investigative disposition is critical as research moves from passive to active. Research in this context is not just an educational endgame of retrieving knowledge, but rather the constant pursuit and creation of new knowledge necessary to enable ideational and prototyping growth toward innovation or invention through creative practice. The transformational dynamic of *assets to access* comes into play here. Developing an intrinsically motivated investigative disposition in a highly interactive culture of collaborative creativity implies accessing living resources and engaging these resources in continuous dialogue. Gloor's (2017) concept of collaborative innovation networks embodies this connected, living-expert research and feedback resource that can be created to surround and enhance creative production.

Ideation development speaks to the growth and development of the capacity to generate ideas.

Experimentational development is the growth and development of the capacity to prototype ideas and to test them in the currency or medium of the discipline or field where the creative initiative is taking place. Ideation development and experimentational development go hand in hand, because they are both generative: a learner can generate new ideas through thought process and the application of imagination, as well as by testing ideas through experimentation, which provides feedback (new ideas) for further prototyping. Although they are interconnected generative strands, I have distinguished them from each other in an educational development context because moving from thought to form in creative practice can prove difficult for many learners. In ideation, learners can have difficulty engaging in divergent thinking, where they generate numerous alternatives as potential problem resolutions. They can also experience issues engaging in convergent thinking, where they have to decide among ideas for problem resolution and ultimately prototyping. It is one thing for a learner to operate in the thought realm of imagination to generate ideas; it is another to bring thoughts to form, so ideas can be tested as prototypes. Anyone involved in educational practice can easily recall in their experience both learners and educators who have lots of ideas that generate little or no actual creative production. Anxiety often accompanies the process of actually trying out one's ideas. It is great to have lots of ideas for the plot structure of your first novel, but eventually you have to sit down and write something if you want to produce something. Ideation development combined with experimentational development represents the core dynamic of creative practice engaging in a sequence of thoughts and actions that leads to novel, adaptive production (Lubart, 2000). The high interactivity and positivity of an educational culture of collaborative creativity amplifies the generative aspects of both ideation and experimentational development. Empathetic and generative listening is conducive to the proliferation of ideas in the thought realm of imagination, and also conducive to further generation of ideas through feedback loops focused on prototype experimentation.

Discipline-complexity development is the growth and development of the capacity to accumulate increasingly more complex domain-relevant knowledge and skills specific to a creative endeavour.

Critical thinking development is closely related with discipline-complexity development. It involves effective synthesis and analysis of all gathered and generated information and alternatives to inform decisions throughout the creative process. There is constant need to assess the quality and efficacy of alternatives produced through the generative processes of ideation and experimentation. Against the backdrop of easy access to massive volumes of information, critical thinking development is key in creative practice, to assess the value and quality of available data and knowledge from the diverse sources now available for knowledge retrieval.

It is important to note that the relationship of the strands of discipline-complexity development and critical thinking development to broader educational design is different within an educational culture of collaborative creativity. In more traditional knowledge-acquisition-and-retention educational configurations, domain-relevant knowledge acquisition and critical thinking development are endgames in themselves. In an educational ecosystem of collaborative creativity, however, these strands serve creative production, giving the strands a meaningful and relevant context for learners as learners engage them for creative production. The acquisition of knowledge and corresponding critical thinking skills are far different in an intrinsically motivated, highly interactive and supportive collaborative culture, where there is a real-world need for knowledge acquisition and its critical assessment to fuel learner-owned or co-owned innovation and invention.

Creative sustain development refers to the development of the capacity to engage in increasingly more sophisticated and sustained sequences of idea generation and prototyping over time, against a backdrop of greater discipline complexity, toward original research and production. Imagine comparing an 8-year-old learner writing an original story that is perhaps 250 words to an experienced adult novelist writing a book of 100,000 words with sophisticated plot and character development. Both are creating original work. The young learner is creating original work gauged from a personal/historical perspective. The work of the adult novelist is viewed through the sociocultural lens. The longitudinal rigour and complexity of the adult work is much greater than that of the young learner. The adult work goes through innumerable iterations of revisions and prototyping over extended periods of time. Think of new scientific developments that take years of research, experimentation, and feedback through extensive collaborative networks to produce viable inventive results. The capacity to sustain a creative endeavour through recurrent iterations of ideation and prototyping over time is a significant indicator of heightened creative capacity and creative maturity. Collaborative educational cultures are conducive to enabling growth in creative sustain capacity, because their high levels of interactivity provide high volumes of ideation and feedback that are the lifeblood of increasingly complex creative initiatives. Also, from a perspective of practical educational application, a learner's ideation and prototyping journeys through creative production can be mapped as developmental evidence to serve learning-experience and assessment design, as well as mentoring tactics and strategies.

Learning-Experience Design and Assessment Design Considerations for Collaborative and Creative Development

In an educational culture of collaborative creativity, learning-experience design and assessment design are informed by the creative development framework. Many educational jurisdictions have formally embraced creativity and collaboration as competencies in 21st century learning. This is well intended, but unless creativity and collaboration are applied in a *new* educational ecosystem focused on creative development through collaboration, they stand to lose their most transformative potential by solely serving curriculum content acquisition. Learning-experience design and assessment design for creative development is covered extensively in my 2016 volume *Creative Development: Transforming Education through Design Thinking, Innovation, and Invention.* Figure 7, adapted from the 2016 book, represents a modified perspective of a learning-experience design progression based on the creative development framework. The original prototype of this template encompassed three stages in the progression. In the 2016 template, the original Stage 1 (Stage 2 in Figure 7) represents experiential discipline or field exploration that is facilitated by the educator. This is a highly active and interactive discipline engagement for the purpose of developing questions to fuel innovation experimentation and early prototyping. The original Stage 2 (Stage 3 in Figure 7) represents the co-constructed early innovation explorations through inquiry, hypothesizing, and prototyping, where the educator is facilitator and collaborator, co-owning initial innovation forays with the learner. The original Stage 3 (Stage 4 in Figure 7) moves from co-constructed learner invention or innovation to student-initiated innovation and invention, where the educator role encompasses facilitator, collaborator, and mentor. In this progression, there is an overarching dynamic to build a learner's capacity to ultimately initiate invention or innovation. The stages are designed to get the student into this educational space,

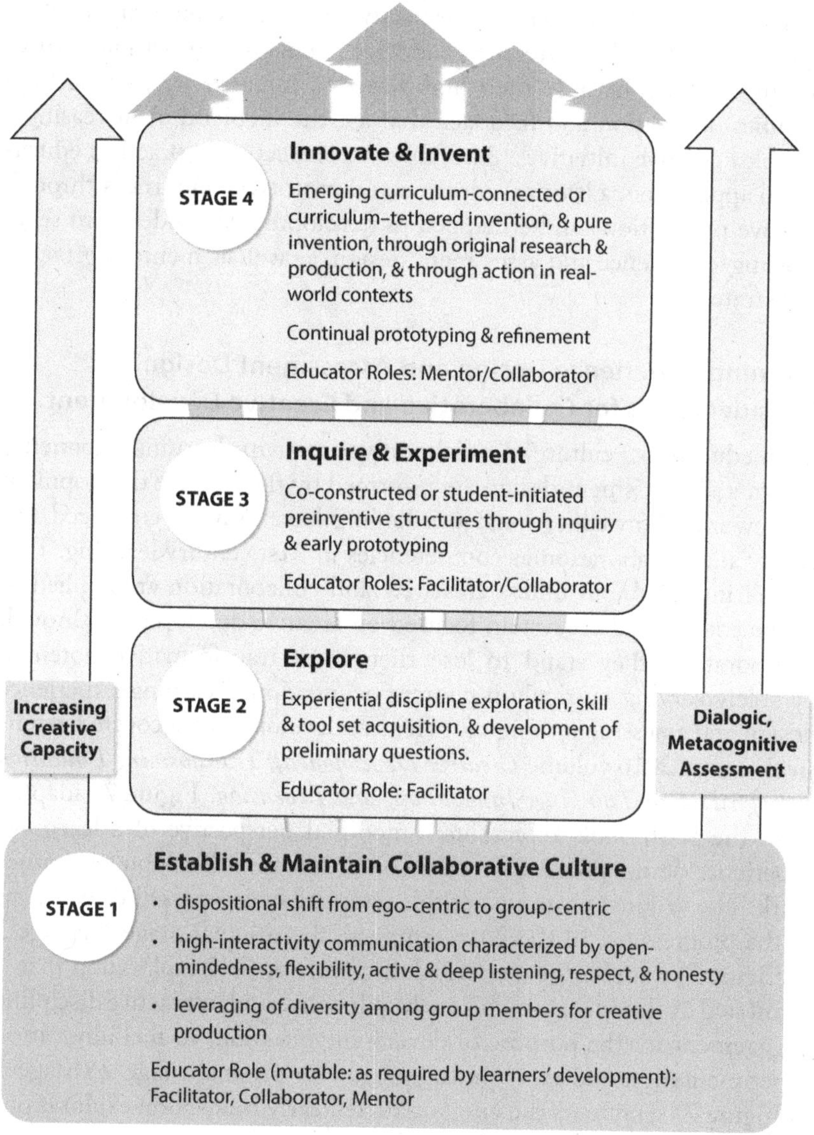

FIGURE 7. Learning-experience design progression for collaborative creative development

which is foreign to many educators. These stages also represent a framework by which to personalize learning-experience design to the developmental level of the learner. The goal is for each learner to always progress to the next level at their own developmental pace. This implies that in any single heterogeneous learning group, one could have group members

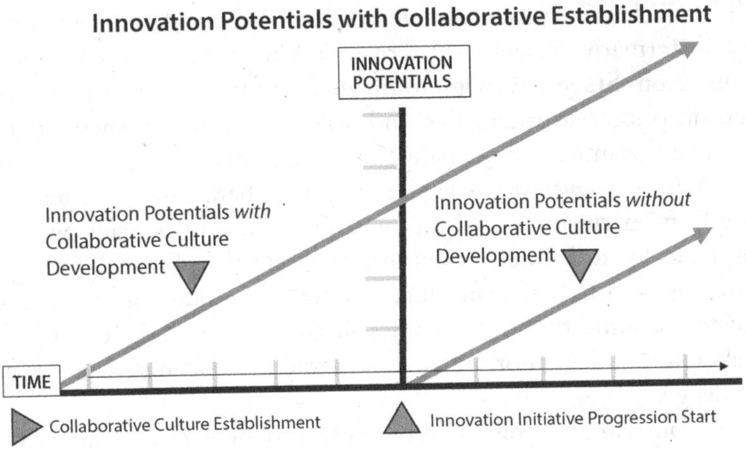

FIGURE 8. Innovation potential with collaborative culture establishment

at all four developmental levels. Figure 7, which represents a new iteration of the learning-experience progression, includes a new preliminary stage: Stage 1. Stage 1 involves establishing and maintaining collaborative culture, which reflects the catalytic and amplifying influence of collaborative culture on creative development. The next figure, Figure 8, represents trajectories of innovation potential once collaborative culture is established. The inclusion of the new Stage 1 was felt to be necessary because of its positive catalytic impact on the collaborative creativity ecosystem. In mainstream educational practice, we tend to jump right into curriculum content or right into a project task. Time constraints on educators are tremendous because of expectations surrounding delivery of mandated curricula. These constraints are exacerbated if educators find themselves in a mandatory standard achievement exam year. Education in this context becomes akin to ploughing through a content field as fast as possible to cover all the necessary ground for traditional assessment regimens. To continue the farming metaphor, in an educational culture of collaborative creativity, a very different approach is taken, because the educational ecosystem is considerably different. The ground must be properly prepared before planting to enable maximum development and growth potential. This environment must be maintained throughout development from Stage 1 to Stage 4. Collaborative culture establishment and its subsequent maintenance throughout the learning-experience progression is absolutely essential to create the communicative and relational attributes that are conducive to the trust, honesty, and group-centric interactivity necessary for creative production.

These collective, progressive, learning-experience design stages reflect the transformative dynamics described in Chapter 2. The progression of learners from Stage 1 through to Stage 4 embodies the whole consume-to-create, passive-to-interactive, and authoritative-to-empowering transformative dynamics. The dynamics of *push to pull*, *one-way to reciprocal*, and *top down to emergent design* embody a deliberate design intention to move from extrinsic to intrinsic motivation, and to transfer ownership from educator to learner, as learners move through Stage 1 to Stage 4. With this transfer of ownership, it is of paramount importance that educators assume the mutable roles of educator as designer, facilitator, collaborator, and mentor, not the sole role of educator as purveyor of knowledge.

The four-step progression represents a framework by which to personalize learning-experience design to the developmental level of the learner. The goal is for each learner to always be working toward the next developmental stage at their own developmental pace. This implies that, in any one heterogeneous learning group, one could have group members at all four developmental levels working alongside each other. Any group could have members who are working on the attributes of basic communication, collaboration, and social interactivity in Stage 1, not only at the beginning of the learning-experience design progression, but throughout the subsequent stages. At any point in time, one could be developing an investigative disposition in Stage 2, through the experiential and interactive exploration of the discipline field where potential creative production lies. This may be the developmental limit of a learner, but the goal, always, is to help the learner at any opportunity to develop the creative capacity of Stage 3 (to begin co-constructing with the educator and peers early creative initiatives across the discipline spectrum), and then the creative capacity of Stage 4 (to initiate innovation and invention from passion areas or learning fields that inspire).

The learning stages place deliberate emphasis on the transformative dynamic of development, as opposed to measurement, which means a focus on assessment as learning and as creative development in the educational ecosystem of collaborative creativity. The educator in this educational environment becomes designer, co-explorer, co-creator, collaborator, and mentor, working to develop the creative capacity of the learner, as opposed to being inadvertently placed in the position of constantly measuring the student against their peers. In the latter orientation, it is very difficult to develop trust with the learner to create a seamless collaborative culture between educator and learner. Assessment anxiety, discussed at greater length in Chapter 4, is pervasive in traditional summative, assessment-intense educational environments, largely because of the potential of social and academic invalidation through public comparisons to peers. There is no need to focus solely on a summative approach to assessment in a culture focused on development. Summative assessment is counterproductive in this culture, because the educational focus has shifted, from the measurement of curriculum content acquisition and retention, to creative development and the acquisition of increasingly more complex creative and collaborative capacities and processes. This is a transition from discipline-content acquisition to dispositional development that *includes* discipline-content acquisition, but in a very different educational ecosystem. In this ecosystem, the deliberate design in the progression from extrinsic motivation to intrinsic motivation includes a transfer of ownership in assessment. Why should learners always have to rely on external prompts to know how they are developing? In a dialogic and collaboratively rich educational environment, assessment as learning would encompass the following attributes, as described by the Western and Northern Canadian Protocol for Collaboration in Education (2006) and the Ontario Ministry of Education (2013):

> Assessment as learning is a process of developing and supporting metacognition for students. Assessment as learning focuses on the role of the student as the critical connector between assessment and learning. When students are active, engaged, and critical assessors, they make sense of information, relate it to prior knowledge, and use it for new learning. This is the regulatory process of metacognition. It occurs when students monitor their own learning and use the feedback from this monitoring to make adjustments, adaptations, and even major changes in what they understand. It requires that teachers help students develop, practice, and become comfortable with reflection and critical analysis of their own learning. (Ontario, p. 27)

Assessment as learning in an educational culture of collaborative creativity enhances learning and creative outcome potentials. It places the educator in the role of a developmental ally, while equipping the learner with increasing critical thinking capacity and heightened metacognitive awareness in a context that is relevant to the learner's needs and interests.

COLLABORATING TO CREATE 5

Peter Gloor on Collaborative Innovation Networks and the Honest Signals of Collaboration

EDITED BY ROBERT KELLY

Peter A. Gloor is a research scientist at the Center for Collective Intelligence at MIT's Sloan School of Management, where he leads the Collaborative Innovation Networks (COINs) project. He is also founder and chief creative officer of software company Galaxyadvisors, where he puts his academic insights to practical use helping clients to coolhunt (spotting the next big thing by finding the trendsetters) by analyzing social networking patterns on the Internet, and to coolfarm (increasing organizational happiness, creativity, and performance) through workforce analytics.

In addition, Peter is an honorary professor at the University of Cologne and an honorary professor at Jilin University, Changchun, China. He has also taught classes at the University of Bamberg; Universidad Católica, Santiago de Chile; Aalto University, Helsinki; the University of Rome Tor Vergata; and the University of Applied Sciences Northwestern Switzerland. Previously, Peter was a partner with Deloitte Consulting, leading its e-business practice for Europe, a partner with PricewaterhouseCoopers, and the section leader for software engineering at UBS. He was a postdoctoral fellow at the MIT Lab for Computer Science in the Advanced Networking Architecture group, working on hypertext well before the Web emerged and creating the multimedia CD "Animated Algorithms" (published by MIT Press). He obtained a PhD in computer science and a master's degree (diploma) in mathematics from the University of Zurich.

How the Concept of Collaborative Innovation Networks Began

Collaborative innovation networks or COINs are cyberteams of self-motivated people with a collective vision, enabled by technology to collaborate in creating a cool trend—an innovation—by sharing ideas, information, and work. COINs have been around for hundreds of years. Many of us have already been a part of one without knowing it. What makes COINs so relevant today is that the concept has reached its tipping point—thanks to the Internet and the World Wide Web. COINs are powered by swarm creativity. People work together in a structure that enables a fluid creation and exchange of ideas. It may look chaotic from the outside, but the structure of a COIN is like a beehive or ant colony—immensely productive because each team member knows intuitively what she or he needs to do.[1]

My work on collaborative innovation networks started when I was working in Zurich as the head of eBusiness Europe for Deloitte Consulting. During the day, I was selling strategy consulting, and, at night, we developed the concept called "collaborative knowledge network," which was much more fun than selling eBusiness strategy consulting. We had formed our own COIN (collaborative innovation network), only I didn't call it that at that time. We found this concept very powerful. It took us a year. It was before technologies such as Zoom and WebEx: we used a very early technology called eRoom to have virtual meetings—"virtual block backs," we called them—which occurred once every other week with about 10 people. The team included the instigator from New York, people from Amsterdam, from San Francisco, from Melbourne, Australia. That means somebody always had to wake up in the middle of the night, but we were so passionate! We were forming that COIN, and we were building our offering—which, in consulting, basically means fancy PowerPoint slide decks. Even then, we built this array tool where we were collecting best practices and knowledge-sharing and developing the benchmark.

In 2002, I left Deloitte and went to MIT. Deloitte allowed me to take my own e-mail for analysis. I'm a really stubborn person. I started with my own networks and, at the same time in parallel, I used the World Wide Web consortium archive, because that was available online and I had experienced it firsthand, so it was my blueprint in the open source world. The Web consortium archive came from the same team that I had been part of as a postdoctoral fellow at MIT ten years before, in 1991. We built our very first social network analysis tool. I recruited some students, who were much better coders than I was, to write the software, because you could not really take e-mail. At that time, there was no tool at all that worked. Then, my research basically consisted of observing network usage. I found that they looked like fully-connected astronomical groups where the core COIN (collaborative innovation network) is surrounded by the galaxy of the CLN (collaborative learning network) and then the asteroid belts of the CIN (collaborative interest network), and that's how everything began

Other strands also influenced the work. My father was a civil engineer. He always had a lot of bees. I grew up with bees, and he was always telling me how wonderfully social they are, and how they self-organize and can do wonderful things. This impacted how I looked at my collaborative knowledge networks, and it was the time when these networks were the very first communities of practice. There was also my computer science background calling me into this space, with all of those swarm-based computer science algorithms. Another strand is that my family is full of teachers—my very first job was as a math teacher, my grandfather was a principal of a town school in Switzerland. Teaching involves very self-organizing networks. So, that's what taught me the learning part and the learning-community part.

I was very infused with bee stuff and with learning stuff. I combined all of this together. As an aside, as a boy, I wasn't happy with the bees. We always had to help getting the honey out. It was a lot of work and they were stingy. They were stinging us. I had no choice.

The Honest Signals of Collaboration

Our research has focused on studying hundreds of communication archives of organizations to develop an understanding of the patterns of communication among team members that support creativity, collaboration, and communication. We identified communication patterns that are indicative of higher functioning teams in these areas.

CENTRAL LEADERSHIP AND ROTATING LEADERSHIP

The first honest signals of collaboration are strong leadership and rotating leadership. At the time when I was starting the work on COINs and considering my background working with bees, I thought that all bees are equal. But what I learned and realized is that, in the beehive, not all bees are equal. There are busy bees and lazy bees. Busy bees die after three months. Lazy bees die after six, seven, eight, maybe even nine months. In other words, summer bees that work very hard collecting the honey seem to die young. Bees in the winter primarily eat, and their only purpose is to keep the beehive alive so there are some workers in the spring. With humans, it's the same. If you look at open source organizations like Wikipedia or Linux, you have a queen bee. You have somebody, and it's normally not one queen bee, because one queen bee alone dies. You have rotating leaders, but you have strong leaders. You have strong leaders that are humble, compassionate, and constantly curious. Without a strong leader, if everybody is equal, nothing is going to work, because you will just always pass on whatever problem you have. You need somebody who steps up and assumes responsibility. The leader has to be extrinsically motivated, and they have to be accepting of the fact that other people have other priorities. Then there has to be room for rotating leadership to emerge, because you empower whoever has the right skills for the job, instead of thinking that you have to be in charge constantly. A group of strong leaders taking turns is better than just one central leader.

BALANCED CONTRIBUTION

Analyzing the patterns of communication among organization members can provide insight into the structure of communication over time. It can reveal a central-leadership dominated pattern or a more balanced pattern of communication among team members. From our observation of e-mail exchanges among team members, we concluded that an indicator of a higher level of creativity was when all members of a team had a balanced contribution to a team initiative.

RAPID RESPONSE, HONEST SENTIMENT, SHARED CONTEXTS, AND SOCIAL CAPITAL

The honest signals of collaboration enable us to analyze communication among members of a group to provide insights into the creative potential of the group. More importantly, encouraging group members to embody the honest signals of collaboration goes a long way to enabling greater innovation. The following are additional, important signals of collaboration.

Rapid response: This is the speed at which team members respond to communications among themselves. Rapid response is an indicator of respect between communicators. It fosters trust and is often an indicator of satisfaction.

Honest sentiment: I discovered through my own teaching that honest language means using positive words and negative words. That was a predictor of collaboration: saying what is good and saying what is bad. We looked at creative teams in different settings, including our student teams and teams of health-care practitioners. We used e-mail archives to examine the success of those teams. The ideal teams start off by being nice to each other, then they become honest. So, you see something with that slope. It starts very positively, because in the beginning you have to be supportive to build trust. Once you have that trust, team members can handle honest sentiment much more easily. They realize that honest feedback has nothing to do with them personally.

Shared context: The basic premise of shared context as collaborative indicator is that the more team members develop their own language and vocabulary among themselves, the more innovative they are. We examined two contexts of communication among team members. We found that the more that a team was focused on inventing new vocabulary and abbreviations to discuss new ideas, the more creative they were. Also, when somebody introduced a new word into the group, we would track the diffusion of the new word among group members to determine how quickly others picked up the word. The more team members picked up a new term, the more successful they were.

Social capital: This refers to the resources available to people and entities because of their networks. It refers to the assets we possess by virtue of the social relations that we develop and maintain, and the shared values that arise from those networks. Higher levels of social capital among group members can be conducive to greater creative outcomes through collaboration.

Starting a collaborative innovation network often starts with a very creative person. This person is highly intrinsically motivated, and they are on a mission, and they want to change the world in a particular way. They want to succeed in recruiting a small group of like-minded souls to establish the initial collaborative innovation network (COIN). Normally, this is a very small group. It's just three to 15 people that, together, turn this initially crazy vision into a first prototype. Then they recruit a larger group, and that's what I call the "collaborative learning network" (CLN) that encompasses hundreds of people. As the innovation spreads to broader society, the thousands of people who show interest in the innovation form what I call a "collaborative interest network" (CIN). The COIN is the centre of an innovation engine that could rapidly involve anyone on the planet who shares passionate interests and who is intrinsically motivated to set the stage for new COINs to develop.

NOTE

1 Peter Gloor. "Collaborative innovation networks: How to mint your COINs?" in the proceedings of the 2007 International Symposium on Collaborative Technologies and Systems Conference (CTS 2007), Orlando, FL, June 2007, xix.

4

Considerations for Establishing a Culture of Collaborative Creativity

Educators are practical people. We are always looking for things that work with learners and that make the day-to-day educational experience more interesting, exciting, and engaging for everyone. The challenges faced by educators across disciplines and developmental levels are quite profound. Cultural diversity, educational diversity, making remote curriculum content relevant, and limited resources are only a some of the many constraints facing many educators in their professional practice. Inevitably, any educational concept or idea has to manifest itself in educational practice to prove its merit. To fully maximize its potential in a developmental educational environment, collaborative creativity has to be understood from a research/theoretical perspective all the way to implementation in educational practice as cultural transformation. It is not enough to take the concept of collaboration and retrofit it onto traditional educational discourses largely focused on delivery of curriculum content and retention. Retrofitting confers some benefit, but they skew toward traditional, standardized educational cultures limits the impact and depth of any collaborative development initiative. Collaborative development requires a meaningful context. Think of a flower garden metaphor. Many flowers in a garden could grow in marginal environments on their own. But the garden fosters the flowers by increasing the positive variables that are available to the plants, such as sunlight, water, and soil nutrients. The more positive variables available, the greater the probability the plants will reach their full potential in growth, flowering, and fruit and seed production. Bringing collaborative development into an educational environment that is designed around cooperation and compliance will perhaps have some positive effect in creating pockets of collaborative behaviour, but collaborative development will be limited because it has no substantial, sustained, meaningful context to grow in. The creative development framework describes the ecosystem of an educational environment that enables collaborative creativity and corresponding creative development to grow to its highest potential for the learner.

In this chapter, we examine the many considerations that go into the design and implementation of a collaborative culture, paying close attention to issues arising from transitioning from traditional educational discourses to an educational culture of collaborative creativity. This is followed by Chapter 5, "Giant Lobsters, Whales, and Elephants: A Case Study in Developing an Educational Culture of Collaborative Creativity," that provides an example of what this could look like in teacher education. Chapter 5 explores the implementation of collaborative educational culture through the voices of graduate students from diverse educational backgrounds as they tackle a large-scale design challenge, which is part of my graduate program in education entitled Collaborative Creativity & Design Thinking for Innovation.

When we transition into a new way of doing, we have to examine the ways of doing that we already know that inform how we go about our day-to-day business. It is important to identify habits and behaviour patterns that run counter to our intent, and that could potentially undermine a transition from a consumptive, knowledge-transfer education culture of standardization to an educational culture of collaborative creativity. So many times in our professional practice in education, we have wonderful new ideas to implement that are brought in with great enthusiasm only to wither over time, often without us being aware of the counterproductive skews that undermine the transition. Identifying these transition-limiting skews is essential in the resocialization or reframing process necessary for culture transition. In Kelly (2012, 2016), I describe many of these factors, which are so important to know because they are design constraints that inform the development of the cultural transition program of collaborative creativity for educators featured in Chapter 5. The following is a review of these factors and their implications for cultural transition.

Factors That Limit Culture Transition

Outcomes known and early closure: In standardized, content-transfer educational practice, much of the learning-experience verification is around outcomes that are already known. We seek verification that the learner has retained knowledge consistent with curricular premises and predetermined achievement levels. It is not uncommon for learners to seek out what is on the test or to ask a teacher, "Is this what you want?"

Educators and learners in this context become socialized into a disposition of extreme convergence, because there is no reason to be adventurous and experimental in a predetermined right-answer culture. In collaborative creativity, convergent thinking is important, but only as part of the divergent thinking/convergent thinking recurrent pulse of design practice. A disposition of extreme convergence is a strong current flowing against the development of divergent thinking, which is so critical in creative practice. It is also characterized by early closure in ideation, although the opposite practice of deferred outcome is required through divergent thinking to generate alternatives that fuel the creative process.

Extrinsic motivation and dissociation: In mainstream, standardized educational discourses, learners spend much of their time in an extrinsic-motivation orientation. They experience wave after wave of curricular content thrown at them. The content may or may not be interesting to them. Certainly, many innovative educators work very hard to make all of the mandatory concepts exciting and engaging for students. The issue here, however, is around ownership. In Chapter 3, I discussed estimations of learner time spent in an intrinsic orientation and extrinsic orientation throughout their educational journey from early childhood education to the graduate postsecondary level. Much of the time is spent in the extrinsic-motivation orientation, where educator, institutional, and societal expectations provide much of the impetus for learning engagement and task completion. The critical mass of learning-experience design is not built around the development of intrinsic motivation, even though intrinsic motivation is expected from every learner. The transfer of learning ownership, and engendering student-initiated invention or innovation, is quite often marginalized to the periphery of this mainstream educational culture. The longer the time a learner spends in an extrinsic-motivation orientation, the greater the risk to the learner of dissociating from this kind of educational practice. Dissociation involves emotional detachment from a system that is very predictable, that requires passive compliance and cooperation to function smoothly, and that provides limited opportunity for student ownership. Little space is available to develop intrinsic orientation. Learning is important and relevant to the learner when they see it as important to themselves, and when they have a voice and are empowered to initiate. They are able to invest in themselves and others emotionally and intellectually. They become intrinsically validated. The dissociation phenomenon, which results from endemic extrinsic-motivation educational contexts, leaves learners needing to reconnect in a social/emotional manner, and to learn to give themselves permission to initiate ideas and creative pursuits based on their own interests and intuition, to make the transition to a collaborative culture of creativity. In many cases, they need to rediscover or discover what their passions are, so as to fuel growth into an intrinsic-motivation orientation that is so conducive to higher potential creative outcomes. In Chapter 3, we discussed a learning-experience template intentionally designed to transfer ownership to foster intrinsic motivation as the learner progresses through creative and collaborative capacity stages.

Assessment anxiety and hypercompetition: Assessment is perhaps the most anxiety-producing aspect of traditional education. It is likely the most common point of contention between learner and educator throughout the educational journey. Anticipation of test scores, and comparisons to peers and standardized levels of achievement, can cause incredible levels of anxiety from so many perspectives. No one wants to look bad or stupid in public compared to others. No one wants to be branded as a failure, which can be internalized to become one's social valuation. Traditional assessment regimens tied to standardized curricula and achievement levels that primarily revolve around content transfer and retention inadvertently put considerable emotional distance between the educator and learner despite the best intentions of the educator. The educator is placed in the position of measuring the progress of the learner against standardized norms. A collateral perception that can be developed by the learner in this assessment context is that they are being judged, potentially leading to mistrust and resentment of the system, and mistrust of educators. As achievement is illustrated through vertical comparisons against standardized levels, those placing at the very top of these achievement levels, A+ or A, are the participants who receive the greatest validation for success in this system. This leads to an educational climate of hypercompetition, and the commodification and ownership of knowledge, where sharing knowledge with others could result in competitive disadvantage. This competitive environment can lead to mistrust: any peer or colleague is perceived as a competitor instead of a collaborator. This is counterproductive to an educational culture of collaborative creativity, where a free flow and sharing of ideas is central to the divergent/convergent pulse of the design process. The development of trust through active and deep listening is absolutely necessary for this process to flourish. Gardner (2016) speaks to the potential negative impact of performance pressure in a competitive culture:

> Performance pressure can be a double-edged sword. Although it motivates people to ramp up their efforts, they may also inadvertently

> react in ways that are ultimately counterproductive. In particular they may retreat and pull back to their respective comfort zones. (p. 124)

She goes on to add that collaboration and innovation suffer as a result of this. Retreating to one's comfort zone increases potential for dissociation and increased risk aversion. This also fuels a pervasive fear of failure in these environments.

Fear of failure: When we engage in recurrent iterations of idea generation and prototyping in the design process, failure is anticipated. We do our best to resolve whatever our design problem is through the development of a prototype, but there are always unanticipated design issues that arise when we test out our ideas by actually building or making something. Anyone with high creative capacity knows this. The well-known mantra of the international design firm IDEO, "fail early, fail often," reflects this very expected and natural part of the design process. In traditional educational culture of quantifiable measures of success, an F grade is failure in its worst sense, because it represents the lowest possible measure of success compared to others. Second City's Leonard and Yorton (2015) describe the need to change this perception of failure: "Too often we are told that failure is not an option. But the opposite is true. It is vital to give failure a role in your process. The biggest threat to creativity is fear, especially fear of failure. By deflating the negative power of failure, you erode fear, and allow creativity to flourish" (p. 16). In design classes, I often assign F+ as a grade (in fun) to reinforce the notion that failure in the design process is a good thing on the way to problem resolution. I have often wondered, as a parent, how a parent would react to a bunch of grades of F+ on their child's report card. How could you get angry at this child? They have failed often and they have failed well!

The machine bureaucracy: It is not the intention of educators and administrators in mainstream, traditional educational practice in public education to invalidate learners or to instill anxiety in learners: they are in the public service and have committed their professional lives to the care and well-being of others. The organizational model of the machine bureaucracy and standardized curricular levels, with a disproportionate focus on knowledge acquisition and retention and its corresponding assessment, is by design inherently predisposed to high learner alienation and dissociation. Ironically, high achievers and every student in this traditional educational discourse are woefully shortchanged, because they are not equipped with the large toolkit that allows full participation in an ecosystem of collaborative creativity. As mentioned in a previous chapter, one cannot make the assumption that high levels of knowledge acquisition and retention equates to high creative capacity. Cirque du Soleil's Welby Altidor (2017) speaks to making collaborative and creative capacity assumptions:

> My first major error was to assume that because we were part of a collective, that we formed a community, the "Cirque du Soleil team," we were collaborative by default, naturally. I didn't realize then that collaboration happens by design, through intent and creative construction. I had falsely merged team and teamwork, community and collective work, colleagues and collaboration as one and the same. (p. 75)

By not transitioning to an educational culture of collaborative creativity, we have collectively underachieved in equipping learners and educators to be empowered through increasing creative capacity in a developmental collaborative culture. That is a highly interactive culture, intellectually and emotionally connected, where the educator as designer is on the learner's side of the fence as a collaborator and mentor.

Characteristics of a Developing Collaborative Culture

How do we know when we have created a truly collaborative creative culture? How do we know that the collaborative group is working to its greatest potential? Let us start with the fundamental premise that, when coming together as a group to create something new or novel, we put ourselves in a position to create something that may be next to impossible to create as an individual. This starts out with a lot of promise. Two heads are better than one. Think about the potential of thirty minds coming together to solve a problem. How about hundreds or thousands of minds? Getting into that space of maximum potential will require intentional design of building blocks to enable this, otherwise it remains as only potential and will not result in creative outcomes.

Shared Vision and Leveraging Diversity

One of the major characteristics of a group focused on collaborative creativity is a shared vision, understanding, and purpose. Sawyer (2017) describes two contexts for establishing shared goals: an extrinsically initiated, creative problem-solving context such as a business environment; and an intrinsically driven, problem-finding context such as improvisational jazz, where musicians working together "have to find and define the problem as they are solving it" (p. 51). Gloor (2017) corroborates the importance of shared context: it is a signifier of collaboration, even to the point of groups developing their own vocabulary specific to their innovation initiative. It's exciting to think of the potential of a large number of people coming together for a common goal or purpose. Getting to this point, where group members move from an ego-centric orientation to a group-centric orientation of unity, is not necessarily an easy task.

Former theatre director Ian Prinsloo speaks to striking a delicate balance among group members who are very assertive and group members who work to diminish group dissent (see Collaborating to Create 1, in this book). Leonard and Yorton (2015) describe overly assertive group members as "taking up too much space" and overly compliant members, who default to total unity by not asserting themselves, as "leaving too much space for others." Prinsloo contends that it is important for group members to assert themselves, otherwise the group is in danger of not leveraging the strengths of each member, which is so important to realizing the creative potential of the group. Page (2007) emphasizes how leveraging diversity in design groups is as important as the presence of expert resources for maximizing creative outcomes. Sawyer (2017) stresses how important it is for group members to have a clear understanding of the group's goals. On the surface, individual assertion and collective unity seem like polar opposites in a group dynamic. These are not mutually exclusive processes, however: the group has to evolve developmentally to embrace diverse views while maintaining a shared vision and purpose. Second City's Leonard and Yorton (2015) describe this through the lens of the collaborative ensemble: "Building a great ensemble allows you to take individual differences—even divergent points of view—and incorporate them in such a complementary way that the ensemble functions even better together than individuals do on their own" (p. 55). Overassertion in a group, taken to an extreme, can have a negative effect on creative outcomes. Leonard and Yorton (2015) add, "The need to be right, among individuals, institutions, and organizations, is one of the biggest barriers to an ensemble approach to creativity and innovation" (p. 74). The key is to accommodate diversity and unity at the same time, recognizing the creative strength of diverse perspectives and the power of unity. Leonard and Yorton continue, "If you can create an ensemble where everyone agrees to surrender the need to be right, you will increase productivity by leaps and bounds. You will create an environment where innovation will flourish; you will also make people happier" (p. 75). They further add, "It's all about recognizing that you are part of a greater whole, and that in letting go and ceding control, you open up possibilities you may never have imagined" (p. 80). Striking this balance between unity and leveraging diversity is an important signifier of the collaborative success of a group and its capacity to realize their creative potential.

Both Sawyer (2017) and Gloor (2017) speak to the importance of collaborative groups having equal or equivalent participation and balanced contribution from their members. The key to this is to identify the individual strengths of group members and to make space for them to have meaningful roles. Functioning collaborative groups that have balanced contributions from their members, along with systems to maintain this distribution of task allocation and commitment, are likely to be successful. It takes deliberate design and effort to achieve this balance—however, the reward is sure worth it, because everyone in the group feels validated. The work of each group member may not be obvious or visible in the creative outcome, but the DNA of each member is somewhere in the creative outcome.

Rotating Leadership in the Collaborative Group

We have all experienced different forms of leadership in our professional practice. Some of us might be able to say, "I had the best boss ever when I worked at such and such a location." Yet others complain mercilessly about experiences with administrators who they thought were terrible for any number of reasons. Some of us have worked in environments characterized by the fear of making a mistake, and the potential repercussions on one's career path of costing the organization lost revenue, backlash from the public, or consumer or administrative penalty. We have all had these kinds of diverse leadership experiences in the workplace. We have to consider the nature of the organizational structure where we have previously experienced leadership in order to understand the transition into the type of leadership necessary in a group focused on collaborative creativity. The majority of workplace leadership experiences occur in hierarchical organizations that are designed around standardization and efficiency. Many of us have likely experienced top-down leadership, where administrators establish and maintain organizational policies and standards. Our work in this context is not largely about collaboration, innovation, and invention, but rather about ensuring organizational standards and procedures are met. The leadership will typically assess the capacity of an employee to do this. Leadership in a collaborative group that exists for creativity is quite different from this familiar hierarchical configuration.

The transformative dynamics of *authoritative to empowering*, *push to pull*, and *top-down to emergent design*, described in Chapter 2, inform leadership configurations in a culture of collaborative creativity. The leadership configuration must be empowering to leverage diverse strengths in the group. The group is no longer performing to the push of an outcome that is known, but rather to the pull of creating something new or novel through emergent design. MIT's Peter Gloor (2017) describes the simultaneous need in collaborative groups for strong, central leaders and rotating leadership. In studying collaborative swarms, he discovered that "there were strong leaders, clearly dominating the discussion whenever they felt competent. The key was that it was not blind obedience, but a meritocratic style of leadership where the one who was qualified best for a task stepped up to it and assumed a leadership role" (p. 93). He adds that strong, rotating leadership also needs to be humble, compassionate, and curious. Leonard and Yorton (2015) expand on this: "It is a principle that gives the group flexibility to allow any member to assume leadership as long as his or her expertise is needed, and then to shuffle the hierarchy again once the group's needs change" (p. 17). They add that "leadership is more about understanding status than maintaining status" (p. 17), elucidating the difference between sensitive rotating leadership and traditional top-down configurations. Rotating leadership is part of a group's capacity to leverage the diverse strengths of its members for the benefit of the group. It is about the idea of learning how to take up space when needed and to allow space for others around the creative needs of the group. The emergence of a humble, compassionate, and curious rotating leadership, sensitive to the changing needs of the collaborative group, is a strong indicator that the group is on a positive trajectory for creative success.

Communication and Building Trust

The cornerstone attribute of a culture of collaborative creativity revolves around the nature of communication and the building of trust among group members. In Chapter 2, this attribute is described as a high degree of interactivity, with communication characterized by open-mindedness, empathy, flexibility, active and deep listening, respect, trust, and honesty. Without the development of trust among group members, nothing else matters: not a shared purpose; not sensitive, rotating leadership; not leveraging diversity characteristics. Trust, developed through appropriate and sensitive communication, is the lifeblood of a truly collaborative group, at the very heart of its being. In the feature Collaborating to

Create 6, Christer Windeløv-Lidzélius, principal of Kaospilot, a private university in Aarhus, Denmark, talks about creating the optimal conditions in a collaborative educational environment for trust to emerge. It is not something that is taught. It usually begins with someone showing trust in the collaborative group that starts the ball rolling and, in a sense, gives others permission to do the same.

In a collaborative group, what does trust imply? For most it would mean that other group members are not going to intentionally hurt me or invalidate me, and that I am in a safe environment. It means that the group values me. It means the group cares about my well-being, and the group has my back if I falter. The people on the island of Okinawa, Japan, are renowned for their longevity, attributed to a tradition called *moai* that exemplifies this very characteristic. A moai is a group of lifelong friends that exist to provide deep respect and support for each other. A 77-year-old member of an Okinawan moai describes it this way: "Each member knows that her friends count on her as much as she counts on her friends. If you get sick or a spouse dies or if you run out of money, we know someone will step in and help. It's much easier to go through life knowing there is a safety net" (as cited in Leonard, 2018, para. 4). A collaborative group that develops this moai sensibility is very likely to succeed in a creative endeavour. A safe environment will allow trust to develop. The development of trust will allow a brave environment to emerge, where ideation and experimentation flourish within a moai sensibility, exponentially increasing creative outcome potential. Sadly, in Western culture, many of us are immersed and socialized in an ego-centric orientation that is highly competitive and filled with mistrust of others on the road to looking after number one. The moai sensibility that resonates with Scharmer and Kaufer's (2013) notion of eco-centricity is very much the opposite of this ingrained socialization.

Trust is built on effective and sensitive communication. A component of this, open communication, is described by Leonard and Yorton (2015): "In these situations, frequent, open, and honest communication is critical to make sure problems are identified and solutions worked out quickly and efficiently" (p. 137). Gloor (2017) echoes this when he identifies the sharing of honest sentiment as an honest signal of collaboration. Typically, in the development of a collaborative group, the exchange of honest sentiment comes only after a safe environment is established and trust has emerged. The initial positive, communicative environment is best built around the concept of "yes and" so familiar to those involved in improvisational theatre. The "yes and" principle implies that every participant in the collaborative group has to be able to make offers, and accept every offer they receive from others, and to build on offers. Leonard and Yorton (2015) say, "'Yes and' has a few synonyms in the improv world. You'll hear us talk about 'affirming and building ideas' or 'exploring and heightening' a scene. There are variations, but the central idea of accepting what's offered and adding to it (regardless of what you may think of it) is absolutely foundational to everything we do at Second City" (p. 25). In developing collaborative cultures with both graduate and undergraduate groups, I use Nelson's (2008) idea of "plussing," where every student is expected to add something to an idea that is put out by a group member. This may be suggesting a variation of an idea or suggesting something totally new. The key here is that ideas are not judged and that every idea is accepted, added to, and banked. If I am a group member, once I know that every idea I have will be validated, I now have a foundational premise on which to feel safe and build trust with others.

This goes hand in hand with developing deep and active listening skills, as described in the four-level model in Chapter 3. Levels 1 and 2 of listening-skill development progress from physical-attentive listening to interpretive listening. When listening skills evolve to Level 3, empathetic listening, trust starts to emerge. Understanding the emotional disposition of the speaker through empathetic listening provides the basis for relationship building and a deeper sensitivity toward fellow group members. The level of trust and comfort that comes from this is conducive to generative listening, a potent asset in any collaborative group. Sawyer (2017) describes several characteristics of effective creative teams, including the practice of deep listening. He discusses the difficulty some have in listening to the ideas of others while trying to think of ideas of their own: "Most people spend too much time planning their own actions and not enough time listening and observing others" (p. 18). He contends that with the right structure and environment, innovation will emerge over time as group members build on each other's ideas. By building on someone else's idea, the meaning of each idea becomes clearer over time as it hybridizes with other ideas in the creative dynamic. Surprising questions emerge.

Developing an educational culture of collaborative creativity happens by intentional design. We cannot assume that collaborative creativity will just happen if we put groups of people together: we have to look at negative socialized attributes from predominant existing cultures as design constraints going forward. The development and evolution of collaborative culture takes constant attention and practice to overcome assumptions that limit or preclude transition into this culture. The initial transition to collaborative culture is the point of highest group anxiety for group members. This will dissipate quickly with intelligent and sensitive design that takes into account undermining factors, while being mindful of the optimal characteristics of a well-functioning collaborative group engaging in creating something new or novel.

COLLABORATING TO CREATE 6

Christer Windeløv-Lidzélius on 1 + 1 = 11: Building Collaborative Culture

EDITED BY ROBERT KELLY

Christer Windeløv-Lidzélius is the principal at Kaospilot, a renowned business and design school in Denmark. His expertise lies at the intersection of leadership, strategy, and innovation. He holds a PhD from Tilburg University in the Netherlands, and an MBA from Heriot-Watt University in Scotland, and a Kaospilot degree. Christer is an experienced board member in a variety of industries, and a public speaker, and from time to time he writes articles in popular media.

What is Kaospilot?

Kaospilot is a private postsecondary school in Aarhus, the second largest city in Denmark. It started in 1991 as more or less an experiment on how to create a school to fit the new world we were entering, with the fall of the Berlin Wall, the emergence of information technologies, and everything that happened in the late eighties and the beginning of the nineties. The school started, in a way, by asking itself: What does it take to motivate students to learn and to create? If people can't find jobs, how can we help them create jobs? This was the beginning of the entrepreneurial spirit, or "the entrepreneur as a career." We may not have used those words at that time, but it was part of the sentiment. The school was rooted very much in the folk-high-school tradition of Denmark, which stretches back a hundred-plus years, and very much in that humanistic Christian tradition that basically everyone is part of in Scandinavia.

The purpose of the school has changed over the years, but it has an enduring undercurrent of positive societal change. As it is formulated today, we say the school's purpose is to foster leaders to fully realize themselves as they contribute to transforming the world for the better. It was reformulated that way because we wanted to emphasize that we are aiming at leaders, and we're aiming to help them grow. Leaders are our primary objective, and we contribute to improving the world through them.

We are considered today a hybrid of two types of school: business and design. A way to think of this is: if a business school had a design department, that could be us, or if a design school had a business department, that could be us.

Collaboration at Kaospilot

When you work collaboratively, you might express it as "one plus one equals three." In effective creative collaboration, one plus one might equal 11. The potential for creative outcomes increases greatly. An outcome becomes possible that you could not necessarily predict. By contrast, when you work cooperatively, maybe one plus one equals two. Rarely do our students work in isolation. I would argue, never. There may be certain projects where they are more on their own, but, in every single project, they work with someone, either students or staff from the school, or clients, or a larger network. Basically, you fail at Kaospilot if you can't display how you have collaborated with others. We often work with projects beyond our students' ability. We engage in projects where there is a gap, where students need to move beyond what they already know how to do. The main strategy for moving beyond limits is to collaborate with others, in one way or another. Certain factors come into play. If you ask what collaboration means to us, I would answer that there is a bit of ethos about it, and certainly also something about shared values. Why would anyone want to collaborate with me, or anyone else? Well, it could be because they love the idea, or they love me, and so on. They may also tend to believe in the same things as me. This doesn't mean we agree on everything—it's more like we come from the same crop perhaps, or we grow from the same stem, and in that way there is something shared.

The Element of Trust

Trust is essential to collaboration. Developing trust is interesting at Kaospilot, because we have students from many countries, and we work with organizations from many countries as well. A challenge with trust is that we normally portray it as something you need to earn. But how do you do that, earn it, the first time you work with someone? Do you work on credit? When a group comes together to work on a project that has a consequence, if a group member fails for some reason, or doesn't engage in a way that meets the expectations of the others, the group needs to show trust. You need to give trust before it is earned. That can be very challenging for people from different cultures. We come from very different backgrounds. We need to be like a field, where we can create some sort of touch points that allow us to do things collaboratively, so that trust emerges naturally.

I would argue that the journey to the collaborative culture of Kaospilot does not start when school formally starts. It starts much, much earlier. It starts perhaps in your living room, when you first google something to figure out what to do, and you end up at Kaospilot. From the time you download the application forms, and through the processes required for acceptance, we condition you to the culture. We give you ample opportunity to say, "This is not for me." So, when students start at Kaospilot, I would say that the trust level is high from the first day, because of the conditioning that has taken place over the course of, perhaps, seven months prior to arrival.

At Kaospilot, students develop social competencies, subject competencies, action competencies, and change competencies. Learning these competencies is an important part of what students do in our program. If you started a music festival, you would probably need to know a bit about music, marketing, organizing, and so on. But your knowledge of the subject alone is not going to cut it. You also need to figure how to build alliances, create networks, and obtain support. You need to get things going. Eventually, someone needs to start building a stage and inviting artists, and things never go as planned. So, how do you adapt to things that happen along the way? At Kaospilot, these competencies are thoroughly communicated, and they are immensely helpful, making it easier for students to grasp specifically what we are looking at. Collaboration is central to all of this.

The Importance of Collaboration

We don't have any claim on where a student will end up, and we are not focused on any specific goal a student may have in life. Students may use what we train them in, and what we teach them, to move in certain directions. Of course, no one leaves the school and suddenly becomes a surgeon. But, essentially, we help students tap into their values and realize their visions. We try to support them in that way. A first big step is to figure out how to unleash their creativity. It's not so much that we *put* creativity in them, it's more that we *take away* stuff that blocks them. Here, of course, collaboration again plays a role, because it's about people working together to create something around a joint vision.

People come here from a variety of backgrounds, and they have a variety of strengths and weaknesses. In our field, on our platform, they define projects that they think suit them, or that they would like to do here and now, although they often don't know what importance these projects might have in five years. What happens, on a very deep level, is that students learn how to bring about processes to support their projects. A subtle part of leadership is how to make people help you accomplish your project, whatever it is, when you don't have any authority over them.

As a Kaospilot student, you don't have authority over other people. Working in collaboration brings those subtle tools of leadership into play. Maybe you need to compromise a bit on your vision. Maybe you need to support others in a different way. You need to find, perhaps, completely different ground. In that way, our school opens up a number of potential interactions, where students eventually make decisions on who to collaborate with, asking the questions: Why am I here? Why are you here? And what is it that we could do together? Our school is a very much a relational school, with a high degree of interactivity. We co-create realities, based on people talking, and then doing together things they have never done before. People don't join Kaospilot because they don't want to work with other people, or don't want to talk, or don't want to expand their knowledge and understanding. The relational aspect of the school engages, I think, something fundamental about being human: as humans, we spend time together, we work together, we solve challenges together, we create futures together.

Collaborative Creativity in Education

To have collaborative creativity in the workplace as adults, we need to start developing skills in kindergarten as children. The earlier we start, the better.

If an educator wants to build the capacity for collaborative creativity in their environment, what would I recommend them to do? A challenge you face as a teacher is that you are more knowledgeable than your students in many ways. You need to ask yourself: To what extent does my knowledge help my students? Where should I hold back and not provide answers? That is tricky. For example, this morning I had a conversation with a woman who is doing our final project. What she's working on is something I have some expertise in. But if my expertise complicates whatever she's trying to accomplish at this point, I think giving her advice based on my expertise will take the initiative out of her. She needs to be allowed to stay on the trajectory she now has in front of her. I cannot just say, "You know what? Let's pause what you're doing, and let me fast forward you 20 years, so we can evaluate your trajectory." My teaching needs balance, where of course I help her avoid the most stupid mistakes, but also ensure the trajectory of her work starts and ends with her, not me. I believe that by doing creative work, you tend to become more creative, and by doing collaborative work, you tend to become better at collaborative work. So, I don't want to stop her creative process: that would hamper her creative development. If I behaved like an expert, I might say, "You should do this, you should do that, it's crap what you have done here, it's really good what you have done there." But I don't think that approach would help her or most of our students. There is something very important about my ability, as a teacher, to read the situation: to put myself in her shoes, and boost the areas where she seems to have good traction, where her motivation and strength lie, rather than just focusing on all the stuff that she's probably not so good at.

Many of our core faculty are not subject experts in, say, product management or innovation or leadership. In general, I would say it doesn't hurt if you are an expert on something. Knowledge doesn't necessarily hurt you. In teaching, though, it's more a question of what you do with your knowledge in the service of helping someone else to grow. No matter what the age of the student, you need to find that balance between, on the one hand, how much you stipulate, how much you prescribe, and how much you set their table, and, on the other, how much you let students find their own feet.

I have children who are school age. They are thrown into mathematical exercises or physical exercises or German grammar. But the application and evaluation of what they do in school leaves them uncertain of its importance, beyond that the teacher says it's important. They end up asking themselves: Where does this really help me? How can I find interest and passion in all of this when I don't necessarily see it being applied anywhere? They don't feel connected to what they are learning. I think my children would be very connected if they could invest in their own interest and passion.

An example comes to mind with one of my children. He was in sixth grade and had a substitute teacher one day. The class was going to do something in physics or mathematics, something like that. The substitute teacher did not have formal teaching credentials, but was very innovative. He took my son's class to the beach to explore the impact of global warming on the environment, and to study the dynamics of tides and water movement. He asked the students to build a dam to control the incoming water with whatever materials they could find. Since the water was going to rise within an hour, they would need to build their dams close to the water, to test them within the time allotted for the class. When, later, I asked my son for the highlight of that school year, he pointed to that experience. He said every one of his classmates was completely immersed in making the dams work against the incoming tide, asking questions like: How come sand doesn't stop the water? What if we use wood? Why doesn't a stone erode as fast? They were all invested in a very real way. It's something about giving students a challenge with real consequences, it's something about play. The learning is very real when students are given this kind of opportunity.

If you want to build collaborative creativity, I think this shows a way. It was a fantastic opportunity for my son and his classmates, because they worked together. They disagreed, they sharpened their arguments, and they had ample opportunity to test many different ideas, because every wave came in really fast!

COLLABORATING TO CREATE 7

Jonatan Spejlborg on 84 Days of Collaboration on the East Coast of Iceland

EDITED BY ROBERT KELLY

Jonatan Spejlborg is an artist, educator, janitor, and cofounder of the LungA School in Seyðisfjörður on the east coast of Iceland. Jonatan is also the co-owner of Heima, a studio and residence for artists from all over the world who come to work temporarily and exhibit in Seyðisfjörður.

His practice is concerned with creating structures that allow cultures, languages, ideas, and beliefs to become more fully apparent, so as to understand them better, and to create a space for imagining other ways, stories, practices, and ideals. He is particularly concerned with what it takes to maintain cultures and ways of living, and who performs those tasks of care and maintenance, and the orientation of that work, not only toward other humans, but toward all things, beings, ideas, futures, and more.

The LungA School

The LungA School is an independent, artist-led institution where we experiment with artistic practice as a way of doing, thinking, and being in order to cultivate, disturb, distort, and transform our notions of aesthetics, learning, perception, and good judgement.

As the name implies, it considers itself a school. But it could also consider itself "a work of art," or "a commune," or simply "a bunch of people." These terms fit as well, and not only do they fit, they seem to capture aspects of this place that we consider essential. It is not enough to talk about this school as simply "a school" if we wish to convey, more fully, the experience of being here. We have been developing voices that stand on all sides of the school and speak to the aspects that they see. And together they form a fuller picture.

We are a small school because that allows us to focus on each individual student who decides to attend. We hope to support the students on their individual and collective paths, and in developing an understanding of the world and their ability to act in it. We do this through the language and practice of art, and we consider this experimental educational experience as a foundation for further artistic practice, studies, work, and life in general.

We are based in Seyðisfjörður on the east coast of Iceland. A mystical village between throning mountains. With bright summers, dark winters, beautiful nature, and, even more important, distance from the rest of the world. This gives an opportunity for deeper focus and thorough experimentation. Seyðisfjörður has for many years been a hub for artists and other creatives, and it is the setting for many cultural initiatives all year round.

We have 16 to 20 participants per program that come from all over the world. Each program is 12 weeks, or specifically 84 days, which is particularly important because we wrote the school as a performance piece with the title *84*. Meaning that it's an 84-day long performance. When we are inviting participants, we're both inviting them into the school, the situation unfolding as we are here together, and also to be part of a performative gesture that is happening all the time for 84 days.

We talk about it as being an independent artist- and student-led institution and situation. We consider it a formal entity and institution—a school—but also a situation, which is by its nature something that is unfolding all the time. We experiment with artistic practice as a way of doing things, as a way of being, and also as a way, in broad terms, of engaging with our surroundings in general. And with this I mean engaging with everything around us, both the material and immaterial, and experimenting with what kind of artistic practice serves the way we want to engage with our surroundings.

At the school, we insist on giving time and space and support, and one could say amplification, to everyone, so that their particular language and their way of making meaning and their way of interacting with everything around them is nurtured and investigated as their way of knowing.

Collaboration

We experience collaboration in many forms during the programs, and I think we've always considered collaboration something that can happen if you do other things right. So, the first question becomes: What is it that you do right, when collaboration happens? At least, this is the first question if the conditions for collaboration are properties emerging from a "healthy" environment.

If we start by differentiating cooperation and collaboration, I understand cooperation as a way of being together, doing something together, that aims for smoothness and the solving of a problem or situation. I understand collaboration to be more inclusive of difficulties in terms of resistance and difference. Collaboration doesn't want or need to be smooth. It is not necessarily opposed to smoothness (though I think that can be healthy, at times), but it wants to be able *not* to be smooth and still be considered in positive terms. It even wants to be okay with not functioning for a while. "Functioning" might not be the ultimate goal here, which might sometimes even be difficult to pin down.

If cooperation comes from a desire for smoothness, I often find collaboration to be born from admiration. Of the other person, their weirdness, their "otherness," which is an endless surprise and difference from yourself.

This also means that collaboration can potentially emerge if you address the cultures of competition and the notion of the self-sufficient individual that tend to be dominant in most contemporary environments, including educational institutions and our culture at large.

We try to collaborate through actively paying attention to the patterns of more or less intentional coordination, confrontation, and overlapping that happen among the different life-worlds that each participant unfolds. And ultimately, my experience is that collaboration can begin as something unnoticed, that then is nurtured through attention and focus and will.

When talking about groundwork for establishing collaborative culture, whether in institutions or elsewhere, I believe it is central to create an environment where everyone involved trusts each other's intentions. If there is trust about the intention, I might be unsure about what you mean or what you're doing or why you're doing what you're doing, but I trust your motives. I think that's a completely necessary condition for collaboration to exist.

A lot of the work for developing collaborative culture as a group happens immediately when everyone meets each other. There are these really small things that we've noticed that matter, such as greeting people warmly when they arrive and picking them up at the airport. It doesn't mean that I'm strategic about giving hugs, but many have expressed the importance of those small things in feeling welcome and trusting toward us and the experience they were going into. I guess this is really just about the implication of details that you need to pay attention to without becoming strategic about them. You can't fake all these things.

In the beginning of each program, we have 20 people in the same room, most of them from completely different backgrounds. The discourse and language we apply in the beginning is about nurturing the appreciation of these differences and the different worlds that are born out of them. And in terms of trusting each other's intentions, which doesn't mean sharing a goal or anything specific like that, I believe that everyone who's there wants to exist in a community where we are around each other in a certain way. We want to live a life there, where we allow other lives, other kinds of lives, to exist. I think those loosely defined intentions are the kinds of things we want together and that we are collaborating on an as a community. What I mean by collaboration in this regard is the daily practice of everyone involved, the small things, the doing the dishes, the noticing each other, and so on, that maintains a trusting foundation. There is so much care involved in maintaining the foundation for collaborative culture. And I believe that it is also, often, out of this work that collaboration grows.

All of that can only happen if the quirkiness and weirdness that everyone brings is embraced. I haven't experienced anyone who does not have something quirky or weird about them. I believe all of that needs to be appreciated, instead of assimilated into the same thing. I don't subscribe to the idea that slowly, by living closely together and working together in this way, you're going to become more alike or you're going to share more things. Certainly, you are going to share a lot of ideas, experiences, memories. But that doesn't mean that you become more alike.

Rather, it is a chance to become even more appreciative of each other's way of doing and experiencing. You can share a lot of experiences and memories, but the characteristics of each individual can grow in all sorts of weird directions, too.

This appreciation of difference is an important notion and conversation to bring into place, because the participants at LungA School share pretty much everything while they are here. They live in a shared house, cook food together, do a lot of the same workshops, develop shared language, shared meanings, and so on. But still, during the weeks of individual practice, smaller collaborations emerge that explode in all sorts of directions.

If I'm to explain a little about the program, I can say that during the 84 days we invite guest artists to come and do workshops of usually one week, sometimes two. The invitation is not to come and teach, as such, but rather to bring some of the things they are working on, the experiments they are interested in at the moment, the questions that are alive—bring it all into the studio and invite the participants to join them in their process. And from there the participants get into their own processes and take things in directions that make sense for them.

Generally, I find that when it works really well, collaboration emerges in weeks when structures are very fluid, allowing for different roles to be assumed. And who has what role might change throughout the week. Participation does not come from the designation of particular roles; rather, roles become possible because of active participation. This makes it possible to play with roles during the program while maintaining participation.

A thing that I really like, and that I find contributes to the potential for collaboration, is that many of the guest artists stay here after they have hosted a workshop. They stay here to work on their own things, but they keep on living with the other participants, joining the communal meals, sharing the studio, and so on. It speaks to the special kind of looseness or informal ambience that you can have with someone in that situation. It's incredible, and we really see some interesting things happening there. The workshops become a way for people to meet, and then they really engage in something after the workshops. This becomes a highly generative environment.

Another important thing for us in terms of being in a collaborative environment is that when it's bad, you need to stay, and not necessarily try to fix it, but just stay through the rough times somehow. And that goes for collaborations among all participants, ourselves included. We can still engage in cultivating a community where everyone has autonomy and responsibility. Our way of looking at our responsibility is to just to stay here through everything and engage in the stuff that's hard and the stuff that isn't. Given how closely we live and engage together over the 84 days, we are all vulnerable in one way or another. There's something vulnerable about being so far away from your normal circumstances, being in a group of completely new people. Everyone is challenged throughout this, because you're living in the same house, sharing rooms, and having all meals together. There's such an intensity and intimacy in being here.

Seyðisfjörður is a town of 650 people. There's only one road out, and sometimes that closes so you can't get away. You can't even see the horizon, and the sun disappears behind the mountains for three and a half months a year—all of these weird things that come with this geographical location. If you have any sort of resistance toward the situation itself, there's just nothing to do. You can be overpowered by the surroundings of the natural environment and the situation. There has to be a letting go of that, just to be here. I feel like participants are all challenged from time to time with the intensity of the situation, which I completely understand. I also think that keeping a certain level of intensity and intimacy is what allows the situation to unfold so quickly. I've often had a feeling that, even after just a few weeks, we, together, have developed (and remain in a process of constantly developing) new ways of relating to each other, and to other human and nonhuman beings. Because we each come from diverse contexts of how we relate to each other, we need to create different terms for what it is that we are to each other here. That is why we created all these different voices for the school, which talk about it as people in an artwork doing a performance together, and as a commune of artists, and more. What does each of those mean for how we can relate to each other? What is the language we are applying? What thinking are we applying to the kinds of relationships we are engaging with? We also know that we are going to relate to each other in ways that we don't necessarily have words for. What other ways could be opened up through new language and practice? This speculation is very much alive all the time throughout the program. It places us all in that uncertain field of what it actually is we're doing and what kind of structure we are in, that is emerging, that we can't really explain.

Collaboration doesn't necessarily emerge because you are friends. It is not necessarily because you are family and have that sort of obligation, either. It's not because you are going to get anything out of it. It's not a transactional thing. There's something about helping someone else out, or collaborating, that enriches everything, that opens the possibility to something unknown—something that I don't yet know could exist in that space. Collaboration for me has a lot to do with acknowledging that engaging in a situation may allow something to happen, when I am not sure what the something is. That is one of the great things about this particular collaboration: the uncertainty of what is going to happen.

5

Giant Lobsters, Whales, and Elephants

A CASE STUDY IN DEVELOPING AN EDUCATIONAL CULTURE OF COLLABORATIVE CREATIVITY

Shortly after the release of *Creative Expression, Creative Education: Creativity as a Primary Rationale for Education* that I coedited with Carl Leggo in 2008, I was interviewed on the CBC (Canadian Broadcasting Corporation) at a local radio station. This book, as the title suggests, argued for creativity as a primary rationale for education, right alongside the educational bedrock of literacy and numeracy. The interviewer asked how I would go about making this transformation happen in education. The answer is not simple, because wholesale transformation would have to occur at a variety of levels across a number of educational contexts. This would encompass many factors, including government-mandated curricula, the organizational structures of schools, school design, funding, the education of parents, prototyping new ways of doing, and teacher education. Although I continue to work across all transformational fronts, I feel the epicentres of educational transformation are teacher education and educational experimentation.

Shortly after this interview, I was doing a keynote presentation on creativity as a primary rationale for education at a university in eastern Canada, in the same city where my brother was principal of a challenging K to 8 school. He was in the audience. When I got off the stage at the end of the talk, he was the first one to greet me. He said, "That's sounds all very nice, but what would it look like in my school? What would our teachers and students be doing? How would we go about this?" He then added, "Until you are able to answer these questions for educators and parents, none of this will mean anything." His questions became the impetus for my 2012 book *Educating for Creativity: A Global Conversation*, where I explore educational exemplars around the globe, from early childhood to postsecondary, that make creativity central to educational practice. His questions also became the impetus for the 2016 book *Creative Development: Transforming Education through Design Thinking, Innovation, and Invention*, where I attempt to explain how this all works in educational practice through the lens of creative development. This brings us to present day and this book, focused on collaborative creativity.

I have been prototyping courses in teacher education around the concept of creativity in educational practice at the graduate and undergraduate levels since 2002 at my home university and at a number of other postsecondary institutions across Canada. Most of these prototypes have been successful, but there was always a need to revise, refine, and redesign with each iteration. This is all part of the design process of creating and developing prototypes through feedback loops, and living the idea of educator as designer, and embodying the whole notion of doing what I am asking students to do. In 2012, I got the opportunity to develop a graduate program in teacher education that focused on creativity as part of a new master's of education interdisciplinary degree program in the education faculty at my home institution. Up to that point, I had been designing individual courses in this field. This presented an opportunity where I would have a group of educators as students for the better part of a calendar year over a four-course structure. The opportunity expanded the element of time as a design consideration from previous prototypes, and time is so important when it comes to creative development. Central to my thinking, and the rationale behind bringing creativity into the centre of educational practice, is to increase the creative capacity of the educator through firsthand, longitudinal engagement in creative practice. Therefore, the more time I have with an educator, the greater the potential for the educator to understand the creative process from an inside, experiential perspective. This form of action research was based on the belief that the creative capacity of the educator had to be equal to or greater than the general creative capacity of their learner clientele to enable an educational culture conducive to creative development. In other words, the professional educational culture had to acquire this creative disposition and a deep understanding of creative process if they were going to fill this educational space in an impactful way.

I was interviewed by a journalist from Chicago after the release of my 2012 book, *Educating for Creativity: A Global Conversation*. Toward the end of the conversation, he asked me what my ideal school, focused on creativity, would look like. My answer was quite simple. I needed a professional culture with high creative capacities across the discipline spectrum that comprised educators who were also designers. I needed a highly collaborative professional culture to fully maximize our creative potential and the creative potential of learners. I think I also said that, if I had this kind of professional culture, it wouldn't matter if we were in a farmer's field or any other basic space. Although I believe this to be true, my idealistic zeal got the better of me at the time, because optimized collaborative creative design spaces in education that architect Prakash Nair (2014; Nair & Doctori, 2019) and Stanford d.school's Doorley and Witthoft (2012) describe would certainly optimize the realization of creative potential in education.

The graduate program started in 2012 and is now in its eighth iteration and third prototype. It started as Creative Development in Educational Practice and later developed into a second prototype entitled Design Thinking for Innovation. The current program prototype is entitled Collaborative Creativity & Design Thinking for Innovation. These program prototypes have served as an educational laboratory to explore how to increase the creative capacity of educators, and ultimately learners. They have served as an educational lab on how to establish an educational culture of collaborative creativity.

What follows is a detailed exploration of the educator/student experience of the first course of the four-course Collaborative Creativity & Design Thinking for Innovation program in the master's of education interdisciplinary degree program at the University of Calgary. This course, entitled The Collaborative Culture of Creativity, is designed to establish an initial collaborative culture among the cohort members to sustain and enhance their creative endeavours throughout the duration of the program. This chapter explores the course through a metalogue, where we hear the voices of program participants as they reflect on their experiences. The metalogue begins a few weeks before the start of class with the online program orientation, and then follows participants as they arrive on the first day and journey with their colleagues through the weeklong face-to-face class focused on developing a collaborative culture of creativity. This provides a unique perspective on an unfolding collaborative culture through the thoughts and feelings of those participating in it. As instructor, as well as program and course designer, I preface the metalogue by examining existing and unfolding design constraints in the architecture of the class and their resolutions. The metalogue itself revolves around the first of three learning tasks, integral to the first course, entitled Large Scale Collaborative Design Project. The class is asked to build a large-scale work out of only cardboard, paper, string, and duct tape that would be difficult if not impossible to build as an individual. On arrival, participants have only four half-day sessions to build the required entity. In previous program iterations, participants have been asked to construct a life-size female humpback whale, 14 metres (about 45 feet) in length; life-size African elephants, 3.3 metres (11 feet) high at the shoulder; and a life-size pod of orca whales, 7 metres (23 feet) long. Each of these large-scale constructions had the following design constraints: the completed work had to be anatomically correct, proportionately correct, and with no flat surfaces. In the case of the elephants, the work had to be free standing and have one moving part.

The metalogue that follows focuses on the class construction of a giant lobster (*Homarus americanus*), about 9 metres (30 feet) long, 4.5 metres (15 feet) wide, and 2.5 metres (6 feet) high. The metalogue is supplemented with visuals and anecdotes from the lobster task and from the tasks of previous cohorts, principally the building of a life-size female humpback whale. Welcome to our lab.

Program and Course Architecture

The program is made up of four courses. It constitutes one third of the master's of education interdisciplinary degree. It is one of many programs covering a diverse range of educational topics that graduate students in education can choose from to make up their degree. The primary demographic of those registering for these programs are K to 12 educators, followed by postsecondary educators, specialists from a variety of disciplines, and professionals from the private sector. The demographic for the Collaborative Creativity & Design Thinking for Innovation graduate program has become quite diverse. The 22 students in the cohort that built the lobster had a large number of K to 12 educators, and educators from the fields of medicine, engineering, business, science, library science, and the arts.

The first two, face-to-face courses are both one week in duration and run on consecutive weeks starting early in July. Courses 3 and 4 are both online, semester-long courses with three optional face-to-face weekend meeting times. Course 3 runs during the fall semester from September to December, and Course 4 runs during the winter semester from January to April.

Course 1 is entitled The Collaborative Culture of Creativity; Course 2, Social Innovation, Human-Centred Design and Entrepreneurship; Course 3, Research in Creativity, Collaboration, and Design Thinking; and Course 4, Sustainable Collaborative Creativity in Professional Practice.

Design Constraint: How to Make the Four-Course Structure Operate Like a Continuous Developmental Program

My primary design constraint was how to superimpose a program emphasis on collaborative development and longitudinal creative development, pursued through a form of action research, over an institution-inherited four-course structure. My design intention was different from typical program delivery in other degree programs, which involved different instructors delivering content related to the meta-topic in a series of related but independently delivered courses. I wanted students to perceive and experience the program as a contiguous developmental program, not as a series of semi-independent courses delivered in a traditional manner. The resolution was to design the program as one continuous course, even though it was presented as four courses for registration and faculty consistency. The key program design element to enable this was to build in two substantial creative-development projects that started in one of the first two courses and landed in the fourth course with students producing original work in the form of prototypes in real-world contexts. These overarching projects are designed for creating original work in response to student-generated real-world problems for real-world audiences. The courses fuel these projects, placing emphasis on longitudinal collaborative and creative development while blurring or diminishing any semblance of course boundaries. Course 1 launches the "personal creative development project." This project involves individuals or small groups creating an original body of work in a personal area of passion or professional context. The project has to be something new to participants, not the completion of an existing project or something they would do in the realm of everyday work. Typical projects include writing children's books or books of poetry, planning business startups, and designing any number of things from a line of baby clothing to an architectural project. Course 2 launches the "group social innovation project." Group members identify a design issue requiring a social innovation, or a human-centred or entrepreneurial-design resolution. They create an innovation in response to their self-generated design challenge. Both projects land as real-world prototypes in Course 4. Both are supported and sustained throughout the program by the collaborative environment of the class and by adding collaborative resources to participants' work outside the immediate classroom.

Design Constraint: How to Establish a Culture of Collaborative Creativity in a Short Period of Time

It was necessary, from a collaborative and creative development perspective, to establish collaborative culture as early as possible, knowing that the countervailing factors for culture transition described in Chapter 4 were all at play, compounding the number of constraints that might limit collaboration. The design resolutions, from a program architecture perspective, would involve designing the right learning experience for collaboration, and somehow finding a way to maximize time, given our short time together in class. First of all, I had to design a learning experience in the first course that created a need for all cohort members to come together and collaborate on something new to all of them. The experience had to come from a situation where participants would need each other to complete a task that would be next to impossible to complete as an individual and where no one was an expert on the task at hand. I turned to an activity that I had adapted from a former mentor, British sculptor Ray Arnatt, called "elephant in the room," where groups in a class would build life-size elephants out of cardboard, newspaper, string, and tape (Kelly, 2016). Ray had used it to develop spatial awareness among his sculpture students. Early on, I had used this activity as a one-day icebreaker for undergraduate students during the first week of classes. After watching the excitement and level of interactivity of the students engaging in this activity, I realized that it was a very rich learning context for developing collaborative culture. I soon began refocusing this activity on collaborative development, starting with small groups of four or five building half-size elephants. Through subsequent iterations, the activity evolved to life-size elephants and orca whales with larger groups of six to eight, and then to even larger forms such as life-size female humpback whales or giant lobsters for classes of 20 to 30.

Three Weeks Before the Start of Class

The following is the assignment that the students received approximately three weeks before the formal start of the class on campus, giving them the task of building a giant lobster.

Learning Task #1: Large-Scale Collaborative Design Project

Materials: corrugated cardboard, assorted cardboard, newspaper, string, masking tape, duct tape, box cutter knives. **Each cohort member is to bring the following materials for the first day of class (greater quantities of materials can be added as needs arise throughout our building week):**

1. 5 flattened corrugated cardboard boxes (various sizes – keep in mind that you are building a giant lobster)
2. 3 newspapers
3. a roll of strong string or twine
4. a roll of masking tape and a roll of duct tape
5. a retractable box cutter knife

TASK: COLLABORATE TO BUILD A GIANT LOBSTER (*HOMARUS AMERICANUS*)

You are to build a giant lobster (*Homarus americanus*) (based on the dimensions 30 ft or 9 m long, 15 ft or 4.5 m wide, and 6.5 ft or approx. 2 m high) during the week of July 8th to 12th in the main foyer of the Taylor Institute of Teaching and Learning. You are all to act as a collaborative group to create a finished product that is dimensionally accurate, proportionally correct, self-supporting from the floor for display, and with no flat surfaces. Allocation of tasks and labour is up to the group. Each person is required to document the development of their contributions to this project from start to finish through video and/or photographic means. The entire lobster construction is to be completed by the end of the day on Thursday.

ASSESSMENT:

The assessment of Learning Task #1 is composed of 2 components:

1. **A group presentation** and **discussion** (15 minutes maximum, your choice of presentation format): This should address your group's response to and reflections on the following questions about collaborative strategy and considerations:
   a. How will you ensure positive communication among all group and class members? In this class, we have the rule of "plussing," where every idea is received by adding to it, either by suggesting an alternative idea or adding a variation to the existing idea. (*Blocking of any kind, or negative responses to suggested ideas, won't be tolerated in this collaborative environment.)*
   b. How will you ensure that everyone in the group and class has a meaningful role all the time?
   c. How will you care for each other?

d. How will you decide what construction tactic or strategy you will use as a group/class?
e. How will you resolve conflicts in the group or class?
f. How will you ensure that your section is done accurately—how will you go about quality control?
g. How should the groups communicate and collaborate and work as a cohesive unit to achieve the final goal?

2. **Individual documentation and reflections:** Each person is required to submit documentation of their specific roles, contributions, and reflections to the large-scale collaborative design project. Keep a daily log. Submit this in two sections: the first is an itemized list, along with photo or text documentation, of your specific contributions, starting with the preparatory work before class; the second is your sincere reflections (no more than two pages in length) on your own growth (or lack of growth) in collaborative development with specific attention to:
   a. your capacity to generate and grow ideas in a collaborative environment
   b. your capacity to interact with colleagues in a positive, caring manner
   c. the movement from ego-centric disposition to group-centric disposition
   d. suggestions for improvement toward greater collaborative development

My design response to the time constraint issue was to invite students into online discussion forums a couple of weeks before the first day of class, to make suggestions to the group regarding lobster data, possible construction techniques, and collaborative strategies and considerations. The following is that invitation.

PREPARATORY TASKS TO BE DONE FROM JUNE 17TH TO JULY 8TH NECESSARY FOR LEARNING TASK # 1 PLANNING:

Between now and the start of class you will need to research and prepare the following two main strands necessary for the successful completion of this task.

a) **Lobster data and construction:** All of the data regarding lobster dimensions, shape, contours, etc., necessary for accurate completion of this task is out there on the Web for you to collectively find and retrieve. You can also buy a lobster for firsthand reference. As a cohort, you will need as much data as possible. You will also need as many ideas as possible on proposed construction techniques regarding internal frameworks, accurate attachment of sections, detail fabrication, weight support strategies, covering and finishing strategies, etc., as a cohesive, collaborative group.

1. Research and post lobster data under the appropriate forum in D2L under "Discussions." Relate all data to the macro dimensions in the lobster illustration in the learning task description to achieve the correct proportions. You will need to research cross-section shapes throughout the length and parts of the lobster as well as details.
2. Research, suggest, and post specific construction tactics and strategies for building a giant lobster, specific to each section and to the whole entity, under the appropriate thread under "Discussions" in D2L. We need a complete free flow of as many ideas as possible for this to work.

b) Collaboration strategies and considerations: The most important task of all is how you work collaboratively as a group and as a class. You will need to address the following questions individually and as a class by posting suggestions under the appropriate thread in D2L under "Discussions." You must have a collaborative strategy and consideration plan in place before you begin building.

1. How will you ensure positive communication among all group and class members? In this class, we have the rule of "plussing," where every idea is received by adding to it, either by suggesting an alternative idea or adding a variation to the existing idea.
2. How will you ensure that everyone in the group and class has a meaningful role all the time?
3. How will you care for each other?
4. How will you decide what construction tactic or strategy you will use as a group/class?
5. How will you resolve conflicts in the group or class?
6. How will you ensure that the lobster is built accurately—how will you go about quality control?
7. How will you leverage the strengths of each class member for the best outcome?
8. How will leadership evolve for this project and what will be its nature?

Interestingly, the discussion forum focused on lobster data and construction was populated very quickly with numerous entries from a wide cross-section of class members. The collaborative strategies and considerations forum, and its list of metacognitive rubrics, was much slower to unfold. In my mind, the latter was the more important of the two, because it was the only hope of completing this complex task in the limited time available. During the period running up to the class, I urged participants to give this forum more consideration. In fact, among the first things we did on the first day was to discuss, design, and consolidate a collaborative plan for the whole group that addressed the eight metacognitive rubrics. The following are reflections of cohort members regarding this period before class started, where class members were contributing to these discussion forums.

R.D.: As the week went on and information about the project became known, I started to worry about how this would work and if I would successfully integrate into the class and project. This anxiety grew when I had a hard time developing an online presence on the D2L environment. Measurements and technicalities (structurally) for the lobster were posted first, which was hard for me to connect to. With being around young children and having lots of time with recyclables and makerspace materials, I thought I'd be more comfortable in the construction area and discussing what to do with our materials. I was also drawn to discussions around self-care and group management. When it came to actually posting ideas, I cannot count the amount of times I typed an idea or comment and deleted it. I was fearful of revealing that I didn't really belong in this group or have anything to offer to everyone. I would convince myself it was better that I deleted my comments, because it didn't really push any ideas or dialogue further. Leading up to this course, I secretly feared that I wasn't articulate enough to keep up with the rich dialogue that I knew would develop. I feared the unknown.

B.C.: Initially, I was worried about my ability to be honest and constructive in an environment where "plussing" is mandatory. I have always been a fan of putting ego aside for the betterment of the group, but in the past that normally comes with a need to provide and take honest constructive criticism about one's ideas and actions.

J.J.: Coming into this course, I had some doubts about my creative capacity, and whether/how I'd be able to generate and articulate original ideas and plans. I equated creativity with art, and because I don't consider myself particularly talented in art, I didn't think I was particularly creative either.

C.J.: After reflecting on the online discussion prior to the course start, I feel like the people who contributed most during this section were

> those who just acted, then informed the group of their progress. It makes me feel like groups can really benefit from the unbridled efforts and ideas of group members acting on their own—as long as these members do not get too attached to their own ideas, but instead bring their ideas and progress to the table for seeding, branching, and plussing. This is a little uncharacteristic for me, as I am someone who often seeks consensus, does not want to offend people or come off as arrogant, and seeks feedback early on before deciding whether to pursue a line of thought or conversation. This leads me back to self-improvement through greater courage to share ideas, greater vulnerability with the group, and greater risk-taking (in the form of spontaneous acting, drama, or ideas) without fear of failure.

There is a risk involved in putting a group of people together who don't know each other in an online forum to deal with a task that most don't usually confront on a daily basis. Who builds giant lobsters anyway? The anxiety we experience at the beginning of any collaborative endeavour, or when we are about to join a new group, is entirely normal. It is certainly normal to question our confidence about whether we will be able to meaningfully contribute to the group or be creative or fit in. Among the first tasks for all participants was to post a two-minute video introduction of themselves in the online discussion forums. This seemingly simple task can cause lot of anxiety for some. Its benefit to the group is certainly worth it, though. Viewing the video of someone you are about to meet, where they talk for two minutes, and you see them, maybe, dressed in holiday garb or with children or pets in the background, is the start of empathetic listening. We get to see someone in their natural environment, speaking about themselves and what has brought them to a program on collaborative creativity. Learning everyone's names in a group as quickly as possible starts breaking down the barriers of fear and anxiety. The video introductions also gave everyone a reference to view if they forgot someone's name in the first days after arrival. As their instructor, I knew everyone's names the morning they arrived. This was so important to breaking down the traditional distance between educator and learner, and to begin to be perceived as a mentor/collaborator and not as a measurer.

From a design perspective, this three-week period of online interactivity prior to the formal start of the class came with greater reward than risk. There was risk that, without a firmly established collaborative culture, the forum could become competitive, with participants trying to contribute more than others, motivated by an ego-centric rather than group-centric disposition. By design, I was more interested in making the forum and eventually the classroom a safe place for the sharing of ideas. With this in mind, the concept of plussing was put forward as the only acceptable way to respond to someone's ideas. If the environment isn't perceived to be safe by group members, there is no way they will put forward any ideas or plus the ideas of others. For some group members, participation in idea generation happens more slowly than for others. This is entirely normal as well. First comes the safe environment, then early forays of participation and contribution, after which confidence will start to grow as the environment is fundamentally validating.

The other reward from creating this interactivity forum three weeks before the formal start of class was for the group to gather inventive momentum before arrival, by generating and discussing innumerable ideas and data, and by revealing the collaborative potential of the group and that the task at hand was realizable. The online discussions in this time period received approximately 300 posts from a class of 22 educators, with the lobster data and construction forum receiving almost double the posts of the collaborative strategies and consideration forum. Both were substantial enough to fuel the design journey. Another positive effect of this preclass forum was developing a feeling that you had met someone, or were familiar with someone, before you actually met them in person. Any bit of leverage that can be gained to alleviate anxiety leading to the perception of a safe environment is a step toward developing collaborative culture.

The First Morning of Class

R.D.: Everything changed for me when I was able to see everyone in person on the first day of class. It was almost immediate. I was arriving and walking up the road to the Taylor Institute at the same time as a few others. The introduction videos and everyone carrying cardboard made it easy to identify each other. We immediately started greeting each other, talking and helping each other bring our supplies inside. By the time we started class, my confidence had grown significantly. I was already reassured by the connections and relationships I had started.

D.M.: I stepped into class on Monday morning sleepless and full of emotion and self-doubt. Should I be here? Did I contribute enough to the online discussions? Will we really be able to accomplish this build? HOW? Having always been full of confidence, these questions and feelings I had to navigate through were foreign to me! I was never this stressed 20 years ago when I last went to university! What is so different this time? Lots: four kids, a husband, large

> house (and mortgage), a full-time job, and online learning. I had none of these concerns when I was in university last time.

The first morning of class is critical for setting the tone and trajectory of the collaborative development of the group. With our time constraint, we don't do formal introductions because we have already posted video introductions. In the mayhem of arrival, everyone is carrying the requisite cardboard and other supplies and looking for a place to store them in the class area. There is a tremendous amount of interactivity before the session even begins at 9:00 a.m. Everyone can literally see that they are all part of the same large task that has to be resolved somehow during a week that starts with a massive pile of cardboard in the corner. There are two significant program design elements built into the program delivery that I feel are absolutely essential for enabling a positive group trajectory toward collaborative and creative development. They are theatre exercises for collaborative development, which begin each day, and the idea exchange, or "speed dating" as some call it, used throughout the week as an idea generation forum.

Theatre Exercises for Collaborative Development

Let's have a close look at theatre exercises for collaborative development. Theatre and performing arts people have always been, for me, a rich source of collaborative development resources and collaborative development understanding. There is good reason that I have cited Second City's Leonard and Yorton, and Cirque du Soleil's Altidor in this volume. It is no surprise to me that Keith Sawyer, author of *Group Genius*, is a jazz musician, bringing an added dimension to his expertise in the field of collaborative creativity. Ian Prinsloo (see Collaborating to Create 1 in this volume) is a former theatre director. They understand the dynamics of working in a collaborative ensemble to create something new or novel.

Many of us are familiar with icebreaker activities or theatre games, which many educators have experienced at some time during their professional journeys. These can certainly be fun. They can get the group laughing and feeling more comfortable. The planned theatre exercises for collaborative development are not games or one-off activities. They are deliberately planned to progressively address a collaborative development need in the group as the week unfolds. They each have a specific developmental context. This is no different than training in athletics, where practice targets a specific desired enhancement. I bring in a theatre educator to facilitate this important start of each day. The following reflections come from the theatre educator who facilitated these exercises.

C.J.S.: The very first day, everyone's quite nervous. They don't know each other. I started with a few exercises that had them communicating without words. They needed to organize themselves in lines and in a number of different ways, by their first name, by their birth order, but they weren't allowed to use any voice or any language. This creates a level playing field or status-free environment, where hierarchies are removed, creating a safe space. Then, I added an exercise where we used words but with little risk, still maintaining a safe environment for communication, exploring the "yes and" dynamic of making offers and accepting offers, which is so important in idea generation. There are numerous activities that can be used in this context. I chose an activity called "I hear you are an expert," where everyone walks around on their own path within a designated space in the class area. When I give a signal, they stop and find a partner, and then use "rock, paper, scissors" to determine who will make the offer to the other to start a conversation. The offer is in the form something totally made up, where they have permission to be nonsensical such as, "I hear you are an expert at taming lions." The recipient has to accept the offer and continue the conversation as if it was normal everyday conversation, when in fact it is completely made up. They do this for several rounds connecting with others in the group.

The early emphasis is on communication, establishing a safe environment, and enhancing conditions for idea generation. The theatre exercises for collaborative development then progress to activities that lend themselves to accepting new people into groups and being amenable to constant change. For the next stage, exercises are chosen to get group members to focus on how to help other members of the group to be successful.

C.J.S.: I then introduced the idea of what to do individually to make sure everyone succeeds. This takes the emphasis off "me and my performance" and places it on "how I can help other people succeed." The exercise I chose was a ball-tossing activity that involves calling out someone's name and tossing a ball to that person, who is standing in a circle with everyone else. We start with one ball and then add as many as the group can handle. I emphasize that it doesn't matter how good you are at tossing or catching a ball. It's not athletic ability that counts. When, as a thrower, you call a name, what difficulties might the catcher have in catching the ball? Can they see the ball coming? Do they have the coordination to catch the ball? Do you have difficulties throwing the ball? What do you have to do in order to make sure the catcher catches the ball? If it means walking across the entire circle and placing the ball in that person's hand, then that's what you do in order to make them successful and complete the task. This

> applies to what the collaborative group is doing for the rest of the day, the rest of the week, and to every creative endeavour throughout the program. The main point is that it's not so much about "me getting my work done," and more about "what can I do collaboratively to make sure I'm helping everyone succeed."

The theatre exercises for collaborative development progressed to encompass the concepts of giving and taking space, and deep listening. The progressive application of these exercises was designed to address the unfolding needs of a developing collaborative group while reinforcing positive, emerging attributes.

The Idea Exchange (or Speed Dating)

The dynamic of ideation in the design process is described in Chapter 2. The first day of class involves the challenge of how to bring this into practice in an educational setting. The group already knows the task at hand and the collaborative expectation. They have a sense of immediacy with the time constraint of the class schedule. They have already generated a considerable amount of lobster data and suggested numerous ideas on construction techniques, and collaborative tactics and strategies, in the online forums. There has been a large amount of divergent thinking. As a group, they have some major decisions to make before they start work on both collaborating and building the lobster. I insist that, before they begin this work, they have a comprehensive collaborative plan that addresses the eight collaborative considerations in the assignment. I have always maintained that the actual building of the whale or elephant, or this case a giant lobster, is the easier part of this task. It is the development and sustaining of optimal collaborative tactics and strategies as a group that poses the greatest challenge.

To this end, I use the format of the idea exchange, or speed dating, as a method to promote the interchange and proliferation of ideas in the group. In Kelly (2016), I describe this in detail. The format is quite simple. The group is divided in half and seated in two rows of facing chairs. That way each person has a partner across from them to engage in a discussion of ideas. Each discussion lasts approximately five minutes, at which time everyone moves to the chair next to them, rotating as a group in a clockwise or counterclockwise manner, to begin the process again with a new partner. This is repeated several times. The rule of plussing applies to all suggested ideas, because the goal is for each person to generate as many ideas as possible for the issue being addressed. In the context of the lobster group, the first rounds of the idea exchange were devoted to developing a collaborative plan for the group. This was followed by several rounds devoted to lobster construction techniques. This one-on-one, rotating approach eliminates hierarchies in the group, and promotes a flattening, status-free environment that is a safe space for volunteering ideas. It is a great platform to meet fellow group members, and to develop deep and active listening. A common misstep in the group ideation process is to go right to group brainstorming from the onset of a design sequence. Typically, the verbally dominant take over in this setting, and many in the group remain silent, defaulting to the predominant idea. It is important that each member of the group comes to the idea exchange with some ideas in hand, so they can engage in any dialogue. The preclass discussion forums are typically filled with ideas that everyone has access to and that everyone ultimately owns. The pressure is then off individuals to constantly come up with original ideas, because they can focus on suggesting improvements to and variations on existing ideas. What results is that the DNA of each group member becomes part of the whole initiative, as that transition from an ego-centric to a group-centric disposition emerges. I use the idea exchange throughout the week to fuel the design process.

The First Afternoon of Class

The first afternoon was left totally up to the group to self-organize on both the lobster-construction and collaborative fronts. The process of giant lobster construction had begun. They formed design and construction groups around specific lobster parts. There was certainly a tension in the early going between two viewpoints as to how to start. One view was to just start building and to go from there. Another view was to create a comprehensive database of all of the dimensions of each part to be built, before construction began, to ensure accuracy and consistency. The database group prevailed. I gave this cohort the nickname "Team Data" for their number-crunching approach to this build. The build-now group had to trust that the Team Data approach would work. Team Data had to trust that their approach would work for the whole group.

In a previous cohort faced with the challenge of building a life-size female humpback whale, there were initially three distinctly different construction approaches. Through group self-organization, each view was presented and debated until the whole group settled on a primary construction technique. This group certainly paid attention to measurement, but their approach was far more visual, relying on projections on the wall of actual-size profile views and cross-sections for accuracy. Other cohorts, who built life-size African elephants or orca whales, each approached things in their own unique way. The life-size humpback whale had weight and size constraints to deal with, but was a simpler three-dimensional form than the lobster. The giant lobster was far more complex as a three-dimensional form, and the chosen data-dimensional approach was ideally suited to the many intricacies that this presented.

We were very fortunate to have one of the best learning spaces on campus for collaborative creativity in Learning Studio A in the Taylor Institute for Teaching and Learning. In the photos at the end of this chapter, this learning studio can be viewed from a variety of vantage points. It was a large space, and every bit of furniture was movable. Chairs, tables, monitors, and whiteboards could be configured and reconfigured at any time to accommodate small group meetings, large group meetings, small and large group activities, and building areas. The electronic and digital connectivity was flexible and extensive. There were quiet breakout spaces just outside of the learning studio. The final giant lobster assembly and display was in the cavernous foyer of our building, just outside our learning studio door. This is a space designed for interactivity and activity. It is an ideal space to develop collaborative creativity in an educational setting.

Reflections From the First Afternoon

B.C.: On the first afternoon, I was frustrated at the lack of progress and the data-heavy planning process that the group adopted Monday afternoon. I was also approached by several classmates looking for support in their idea that we should "just get building a lobster and sort it out as we go." Keeping the group-centric disposition in mind, as well as the idea that people bring their own strengths to the group, I gambled that the data-heavy initial approach would pay off in the long run and that people would join their construction teams once they had finished planning the dimensions. This was one of the hardest things for me to do during the week, because I was very worried that the lobster would not get completed. In the end, however, I think that the data approach was necessary to complete the lobster in a proportioned and planned manner.

L.H.: Once I better understood the concept of plussing, I started to realize my potential for idea generation. I realized that I didn't have to have the first idea in order to add something original and useful, even if the idea wasn't ultimately used. . . . I see the different styles of my team emerge as one member wants to keep talking and planning, while one wants to just get going. I notice the discomfort I feel with jumping into this project without a fully articulated plan for the entire group. There is a level of trust that occurs in trusting that each of us holds the big picture even if I can't fully see it.

D.M.: I found the speed dating activity to be a super way to build on our ideas! It seems like such a simple idea and takes so little time. I may not always have the most creative and novel ideas, but I often find inspiration in another person's ideas. Having the opportunity to share my thoughts on ideas other than my own and building on our new ideas is THE BEST! I have made a note to incorporate this into my own classroom to help generate ideas for my students and their projects. It is important for me to note that the "safe environment" created from the start of class played an instrumental role in my comfort and confidence with sharing my ideas during speed dating, as well as during our large group discussions. If that atmosphere had not been created, I feel that quite a few of us would have been less confident to share our thoughts.

Reflections During the Week of the Giant Lobster Build

Three photo sequences conclude this chapter. The first shows the progressions in the build of the giant lobster as they unfolded throughout the week from start to finish, covering formal conversations, informal conversations, meetings, planning, building various lobster components in various group configurations, and the final assembly of the lobster. The second shows a similar sequence, only with the design and construction of a life-size female humpback whale from a previous cohort. The third shows the final work of two other previous cohorts, who worked on building a life-size pod of orca whales and life-size elephants.

In the lobster project, I was most interested in studying the interactivity among group members as the week unfolded, because the nature of this communication through the types of listening that are occurring would be an indicator of collaborative growth and development. Experience and observation have shown that the evolution of a group's collaborative development accelerates as trust emerges. Excitement grows around midweek, as well, when the form they are building starts to become visible to everyone, and they realize this is actually happening and that we are actually building this thing. The following group reflections occurred throughout the week of tackling the lobster challenge, providing valuable insight into the nature of the interactivity among group members.

L.H.: I often find the roundabout conversations about how to construct something so tedious! Sometimes when I ask a simple question, I get the answer with additional information that I already understand, which is frustrating. Reminding myself that people have good intentions and maybe understand things in a different way is helpful for alleviating my frustration.

R.D.: C. was alone in trying to figure out how the legs were going to attach to the frame/body, the spacing, and the articulation of each leg. He needed help to generate ideas. Idea generation was what I was struggling with all week, yet I joined him and jumped into generating ideas without hesitation or any anxiety. I view this part of the project as my main experience with collaboration. We generated ideas, we refined our ideas, we tested our ideas, we added to each other's ideas. We just kept going with ideas and tests until we found a way to make it work. None of the tasks/roles I had been a part of up to then required as much attention and problem-solving. I felt a shift with the class as a whole around the same time. A lot of people were no longer in their original groups and were helping other groups with their problem-solving. Relationships were deepening.

K.P.: As I worked with my group in the construction, I noticed, when growing ideas over the week, the strength and power of merging ideas together. When working with my team at school, the method often used is: everyone comes with an idea, and one is chosen, and we move on. There is never the time for divergent and convergent thinking, so that we can come up with the best solution/task. Entering the lobster group initially, I was waiting for one person to come up with an idea and for everyone to follow. As we went through the planning process, it became clear that what was going to provide the most success was everyone contributing ideas and just putting a bunch of ideas out there, and then working through and testing some of them. Personally, I grew in being able to first listen to people's ideas and then use them to strengthen my own understanding of the process. At first, when given the task of the claw, I had a hard time picturing the process or method that could be used. However, as I began to listen to others, it sparked my own ideas or allowed me to add to others' ideas. The initial process of divergent thinking is something that I feel I need to work on further, because I often need time to "marinate" and process a task before I can visualize a plan/process or method.

B.C.: Communication is the biggest challenge when making a decision. Several times over the week, I witnessed two people discussing which approach to take, when in fact they were discussing the same idea! I am sure that, at times, I was doing the same thing. I think this is because visions and plans are clear in the minds of the people suggesting an approach, but unclear in the recipient of that suggestion.

L.H.: When I'm tired, it becomes really difficult to remain group-centric and intrinsically motivated. However, this is one of the benefits of working in a group: when an individual runs out of steam, the group can carry them for a short time until they are able to rekindle that spark.

J.J.: There were times this week when I sensed that a peer was getting overwhelmed/frustrated, and I switched the conversation to something that was positive (such as vacation plans or learning about their kids), which I think helped in most situations. I was also grateful that my group mates were accepting when I said that I couldn't stay late because I had to pick my kids up from camp. I tried to reciprocate by coming in early, and helping others with tasks whenever possible during breaks. I was honoured that a peer confided in me about an exacerbation of her medical condition, and I took extra care that day to check in with her to see if she needed any support or breaks throughout the day.... When building the lower segment of the claw with my group mates, the need to devise a structure that was somewhat boxlike and yet not flat, designing a framing structure to keep it stable, devising how to connect it to the upper claws, etc., was challenging yet stimulating. We could feel that our goal of getting this part of the project done was so close, and we were rapidly trying out different approaches and techniques, and getting immediate feedback on those attempts. My focus on that particular part of the project was so concentrated that a couple of hours felt like a couple of minutes, and after it was done it was hard to distinguish which of our group members came up with the initial ideas, because it felt like it just evolved organically from the group.

Final Reflections

The following are group reflections on aspects of students' overall experience during the week. They give insights into the nuances of relationship building so critical to developing a collaborative culture that enables creative practice. They also provide some insights in perceptions of their own professional environments.

D.M.: "Team Data" (the nickname our instructor gave our class because of our reliance on data and numbers for the overall lobster design) evolved very quickly into a tight-knit team or family. Whether it was the theatre exercises, a class breakfast at Cadence (a local restaurant), the impending deadline, or our collective desire to succeed, I felt safe, cared for, and encouraged. I believe I reflected that energy back into the group as well. I do not think I heard a single negative comment from any of us, and that is commendable when you consider the amount of stress we all should have felt (but somehow did not!). What a difference working in a positive and caring environment has on productivity and morale in general!

K.P.: When it comes to my capacity to generate and grow ideas in a collaborative environment, I have become more confident in my voice when in small groups. Being a young teacher, I have often been dismissed because there is always someone with more seniority, or who has done it before and wants to continue doing it the same way. Often times, I did tend to be a ghost, because that is the easiest and most efficient way for me to remain in my comfort zone. Over the week, I found with increasing confidence that I was able to actively participate when working in small groups, and voice my ideas. One area that I do recognize I need to work on is using my voice and generating ideas when in larger groups—I will often default to ghost mode. I think this comes from the fact that, generally, speaking up in meetings with my previous colleagues often opened me up for criticism that was not exactly constructive. In this course, I recognized the environment as being safe, but I still had a tendency to default to allowing others to talk. Moving forward to the new school year, this is something I would like to gain confidence in, as I begin with a new staff and administration who are aiming for collaboration as part of the school environment (fingers crossed).

J.J.: I feel we are very fortunate that our class is blessed with people who are considerate, thoughtful, compassionate, and empathetic. This was a great place to start from and build on throughout the week. The activities that we did, such as the first one where we had to pick a random topic and ask our partner to talk about that topic nonstop for a couple of minutes, really helped break the ice and got me interacting well with many of my classmates. One of the foundational learnings this week was that an environment of trust and safety had to be built before creativity can flourish. I used this idea to create a personal challenge for myself to speak one on one with at least five different people each day, outside of the mandated class activities. I'm proud to say that I was successful with this challenge, and this has helped me make stronger connections with my classmates, which I'm already starting to see in our daily conversations and interactions.

B.C.: Another reminder for me this week is that laughter and levity are essential to remaining productive in stressful situations. Whether this is a funny photo opportunity, playing music in building areas to keep the energy up "after hours," eating lunch with my colleagues to get to know them personally, or spending time outside of class with colleagues to get to know them better, there were plenty of opportunities to build positive relationships during the week. Overall, the more I know about the lives of my colleagues, the better our professional relationship will be. Reflecting on my work environment, the colleagues I have the most difficulty with are also the ones I know very little about personally. I will endeavour to change this at the start of the new school year in September.

B.M.C.: I was taken aback at first at how positive people were being. It was almost too sunshiny, like we were on a Nickelodeon TV show.

> At the beginning of the week, my thoughts reverted to wondering if people were just being nice because of the expectation of "positive comments only" and being able to "play nice" had been set. I wondered if people were being genuine with their supportive comments or just being fake. I am a slow warmer, guarding myself until I feel things are safe, and after this week, I realized how sad it was that I limped into our collaborative team on Monday unconsciously feeling beat-up. I realized this week how deeply entrenched an ego-centric perspective is ingrained in me due to the toxic school environment where I work. Our school is passive-aggressively competitive, and there are a lot of counterproductive skews that produce a lot of disrespect toward teachers, where people feel unvalued, overlooked, and constantly anxious and stressed. This week, I practised reframing how I was viewing people, to move toward the belief that we are all operating from a place of "best intent" and all aspiring toward being group-centric. I found there were a few times when people's anxieties were flourishing, where I had the thought, "Wow! Stop being so rammy! What a b--!" I had to remind myself a handful of times to stop negative thoughts forming about a person which would lead to distrust and dislike, instead putting on a group-centred lens to see the situation. When I did that, I could empathize with them, and see that from their perspectives they were just feeling anxious and dealing with their own emotions that had nothing to do with me. I can only imagine what would happen at my school if people started using a group-centric lens to interact and see each other.

The giant lobster got built, and so did the life-size female humpback whale, and the life-size African elephants, and the life-size orca whales. The number-crunching data approach for the lobster turned out to be quite effective. Trying to create an educational culture of collaborative creativity with some semblance of *moai* sensibility is not easy when we don't live it educationally or culturally. For the remainder of the program, the goal is for the members of this cohort to maintain and grow this collaborative culture of creativity, while developing original work through a personal creative development project and a group social innovation project for the benefit of others, which land as real prototypes in real contexts at the end of the program.

The final assessment conversations at the end of the build were largely not about the lobster, but more about the collaborative and creative dynamics, and the trust, communication, and relationship building that enabled these to grow. In fact, if one had sat in the learning studio when the debriefing discussions took place, one would have been hard pressed to imagine there was a giant lobster that this group had built in the main foyer of the building.

As an educator, it is hard to not be excited and feel empowered about the incredible potential of transitioning to an educational culture of collaborative creativity. If we equip educators and learners with much larger toolkits to enable the development of a disposition of collaborative creativity, problems become nothing more than design constraints. To make the fundamental changes necessary to get into this educational brave space, we have to embrace and embody collaborative creativity and be daring. What is there to be afraid of? Who wouldn't want to wake up every day to unlimited possibilities?

Building a Giant Lobster

Theatre exercises for collaborative development

Theatre exercises for collaborative development

Group planning

Designing the lobster's tail

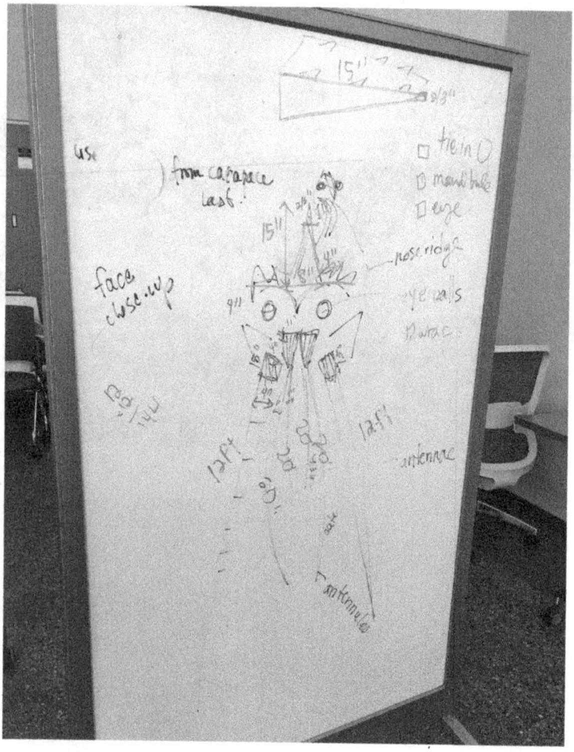

Designing the lobster's face

Lobster dimensions mapped onto the floor

A class meeting around the lobster armature

The giant lobster under construction

Finishing touches on the eyes and antennae

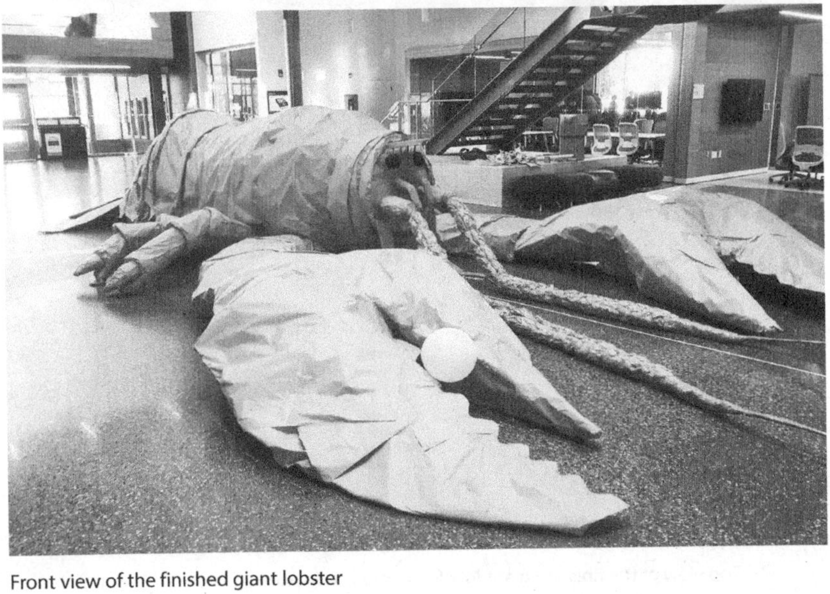

Front view of the finished giant lobster

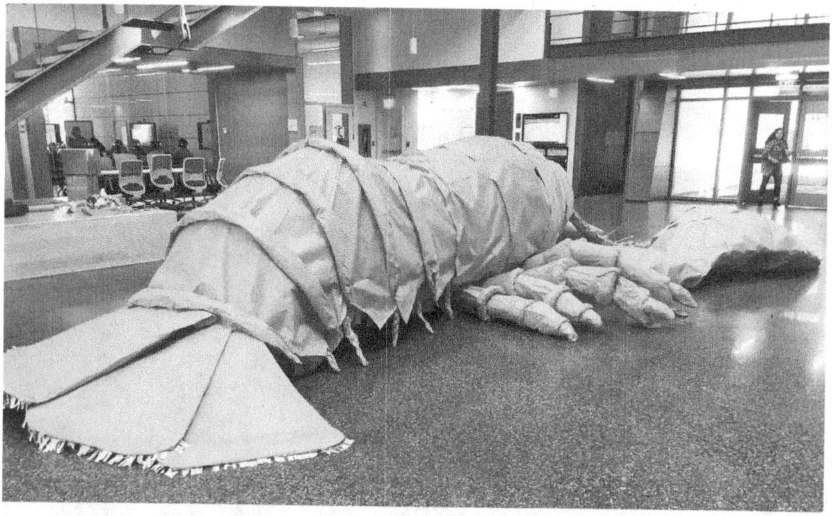

Tail view of the finished giant lobster

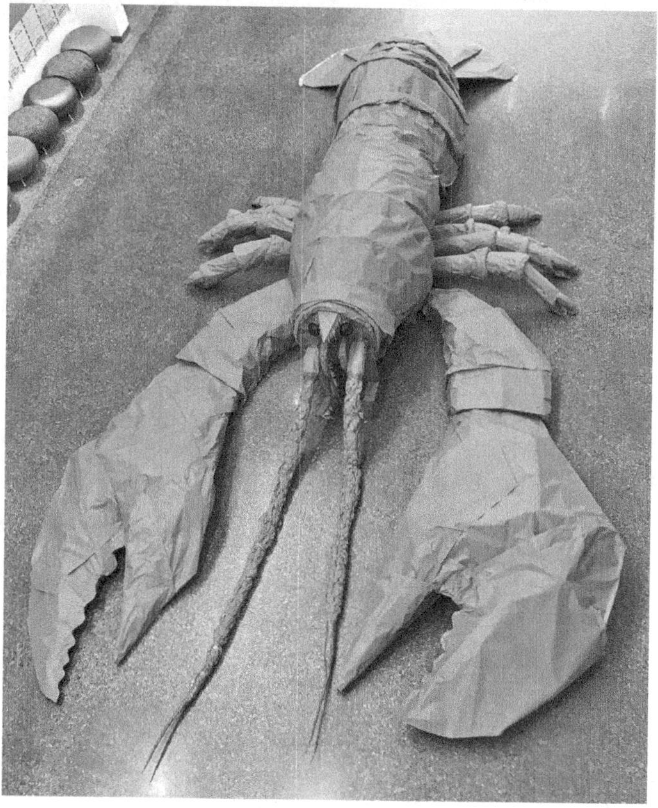

Top view of the finished giant lobster, named Leonardo

Building a Life-size Female Humpback Whale

Planning in the learning studio

Drawing life-size templates

Making the whale cross-section pieces out of cardboard

Building the whale's tail

The whale armature

Top view of the whole whale framework

Placing the whale's eye

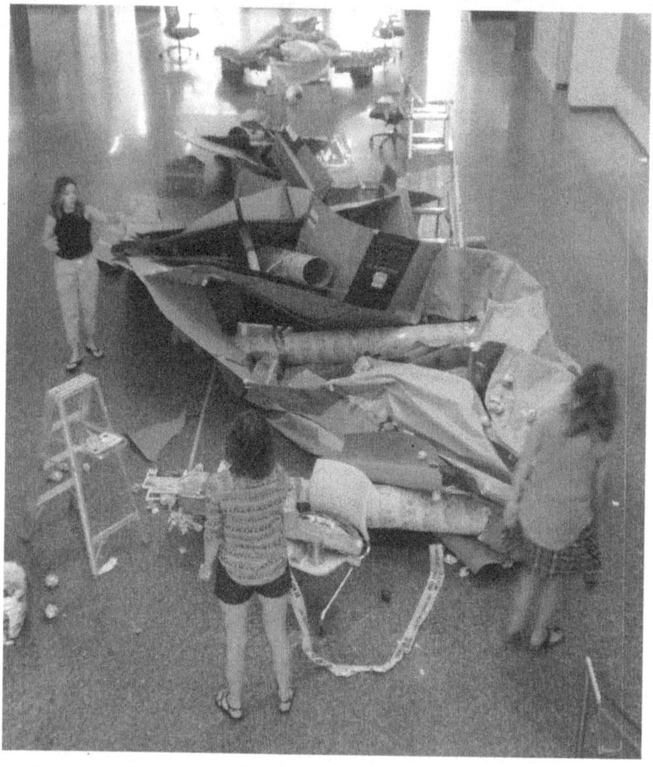

Friday morning: discovering the completed whale had fallen over during the night and smashed into pieces

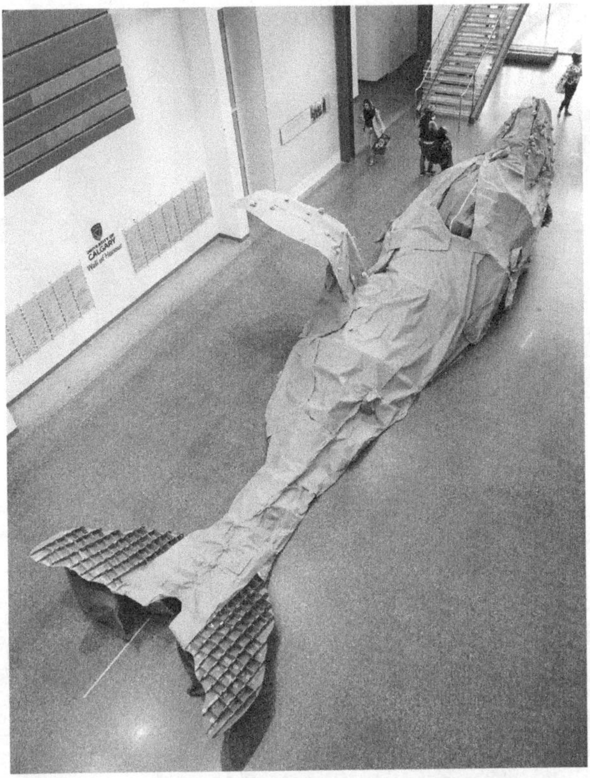

The rebuilt whale as if it was coming out of the water

The front view of the rebuilt whale, named Leona

Other Collaborative Creativity Projects

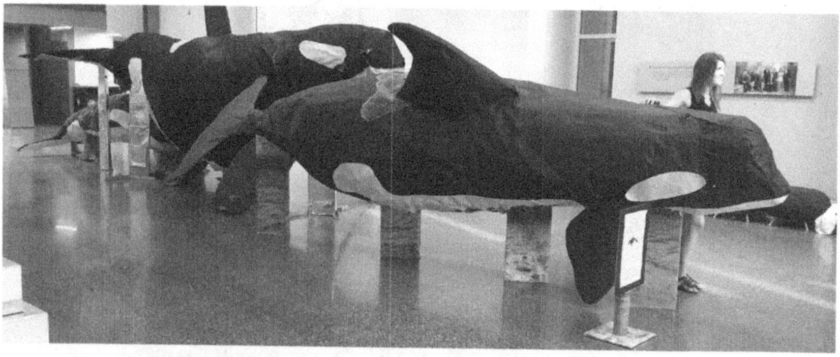

Orca whales side view

Orca whales front view

A life-size elephant

Prakash Nair on the Architectural Space of Collaborative Creativity

EDITED BY ROBERT KELLY

Prakash Nair is a futurist, and founding president and CEO of Fielding Nair International, a leading architectural firm focused on transforming education by design. He is the recipient of the A4LE MacConnell Award, the highest honour worldwide for school design. He has authored *Blueprint for Tomorrow* (2014) and coauthored *Learning by Design* (2019). Prakash's architectural and educational acumen have resulted in the creation of dozens of innovative schools around the world.

The Role of the Architect in Education

> When we think about the "space" that students need for real learning to happen, we are also referring to the social, emotional, and creative space children (of all ages) need to grow and thrive. This kind of "space for learning" is at a premium in our schools. We believe that the design of the physical environment of schools can make this other "space"—the social, emotional, and creative space—not only more visible but more available. Of course, the design itself can only do so much. For students to truly feel they have space for learning, schools need to use the design of the physical environment as a catalyst to change the whole dynamic of a school from a teacher-centred to a student-centred place.[1]

Even though we tend to think about education as a discrete "field," it is in fact represented by a variety of professions, which, to a greater or lessor degree, influence how effectively a particular vision of education can be delivered. Architecture is just one of many professions that are part of the whole enterprise we call education, but it has a disproportionate influence in that it can severely limit what teachers and students can actually do in school. That architecture's potential to amplify the benefits of education has not been realized in schools worldwide comes from its entrapment in its own "silo"—distanced from all the research about learning. It's a self-perpetuating silo. People have accepted the notion that teacher-centred spaces are what school architecture is supposed to look like. So, that becomes a vessel within which all of the rest of education has to fit. We contend that, if you break the model of siloing and if you think about architecture as an envelope within which everything else fits, then that envelope has to, almost by definition, be designed in a way that all aspirations we have as educators can be accommodated. The minute you start thinking like that, you immediately see that the silo in which we were trapped actually doesn't work. It's not collaborative, it's not personalized, and it's mass-produced, which is the exact opposite of what we want. We want each individual student to realize their full potential. Automatically, that old model breaks down, because you're not seeing architecture as a separate silo, but rather as the integrator that brings all these different things together. It's the most visible and most physical manifestation of what we want education to be. So, my role as an educational architect is to go beyond the confining definition it has in schools. In my view, architecture must be the generous envelope that not only facilitates education, but also inspires us to be the best at the things we want to do as teachers and learners.

Educational Ideals

It is hard to debate this simple observable fact in classrooms around the world: that they are designed to accommodate a teacher-centred model of education. Contrast that with the stated ideals of education where, in school after school, the wish is to migrate to a student-centred model. We all understand the simple idea that we get good at the things we get to do often. Dr. Richard Elmore, professor emeritus at Harvard University, puts this elegantly when he says "task predicts performance." So, what do students actually do in schools that we want them to get good at? Judging by what they are *able* to do in classrooms, the answer is "very little." What kind of real "learning" does a classroom actually permit? Students can watch a teacher teaching a class or obey her commands to carry out tasks that can be accomplished within the narrow confines of the 750 square-foot space in which they are trapped with 25 others. What we are saying is that the school is only as good a place for learning as the space will let it be. Our job as architects is to create the proper conditions in schools where students can have rich experiences. When you think in terms of space, you can have good experiences in multiple realms. You can have good experiences by being social, by being introspective, by building things, and by just experiencing life in all its complexity and unpredictability. We're taking all human endeavours and thinking of everything that we as human beings do, from building to thinking to researching to collaborating to socializing to being entertained and on and on, and we are creating the architecture as the vehicle in which these experiences can be delivered. This is a different way of looking at it than the traditional way, where you take a curriculum, and you have a place to deliver it, and that place is predetermined as a classroom. You're narrowing education to the point where the experience has no richness whatsoever and doesn't in any way reflect life. I see education as just a microcosm of life itself, because we're learning all the time. If that's the case, then why should schooling or any educational experience be anything less than life? It's not a simulation of life: education should be life itself.

Creativity and Collaboration

To be creative at something, you need to have some competence in your field. If you want to create an amazing piece of music, you have to know how to play the instrument. While learning the instrument might seem not creative in and of itself, it's the means through which you can be creative. You need to create the foundation for creativity. You can't create the foundation, however, without keeping the end goal in mind: that I want to become good at this for a higher purpose. If the entire purpose of learning were just to become good at playing the piano, then nobody would want to play the piano. However, if one aspires to be a great musician, then learning to play the piano becomes an important means to a worthy end deserving of the hard work needed. Children who can see the bigger purpose will find joy even in mundane, often repetitive, tasks. Children who want to be good as animators, for example, will learn colour theory. They will learn the history of art, and they will learn about animal anatomy to understand how to animate movement, because they want to be good animators and because that's the higher purpose behind all their hard work. If you were to just teach them animal anatomy or colour theory, they probably wouldn't have any interest in it. What I'm saying is young learners will do the hard work, a child will spend three hours throwing a basket at a basketball hoop, if they know they are going to be playing in a couple of weeks in a basketball game. There has to be a purpose. This is something I think is very important in terms of creativity. Collaboration almost becomes a necessity, because most creative endeavours happen in the spaces between disciplines or at the nexus of multiple disciplines. Brand new fields begin to emerge with great regularity from these interactions between disciplines. If you consider 3-D printing a heart, for example, think about all the different technologies that need to come into play for this to happen. I feel that collaboration is a given now in this day and age. To be truly creative in your field, you have to go beyond your field. You have to be able to talk to others. Even within your own field, you have to learn to collaborate. The words *collaboration* and *creativity* go hand in hand.

How Architecture Can Be Conducive to Collaborative Creativity and Different Modes of Learning

In order to get good at what you're doing, you have to experience learning and creating at multiple levels. If you're experiencing information at the level of somebody telling you something, that's one thing. If you're experiencing that same information by sharing it with a peer, that's a whole different level of experience. Or you may experience the information because you're synthesizing it with your knowledge, which is, again, different. And if you apply the information and build something with it, do something with it, that's yet another experience. Architecture should facilitate deep learning, allowing you to apply multiple modalities to that same experience, before it becomes rich and before it actually becomes a part of who you are. By the same token, we don't want architecture to become the reason why you are limited in exploring as many modalities of learning as may be needed to creatively accomplish what you set out to do.

We need buildings to speak a language that reflects MIT's "CDIO" sensibility of conceive, design, implement, and operate. In these spaces, we're conceiving ideas, we're designing, we're implementing, and then we're operating. Students should see that whole cycle of creativity happening, and buildings need to facilitate these processes. Curriculum can then be designed around that sensibility, because the buildings are actually designed to enable this. In traditional architectural settings, you are stuck in a classroom and maybe once every fourth period you get to use the science lab, and maybe on Tuesday afternoon you get to go to the library. Real life doesn't work that way. Our experiences, in order for them to be meaningful, have to be seamless. That's what we're trying to do. We want the architecture to follow the seamless manner in which we as human beings go through the process of designing, innovating, operating, and implementing through continuous feedback loops.

Architectural design has to consider that learning experiences have a mix of 20 learning modalities, which we have identified in our recent book *Learning by Design*.[2]

The 20 modalities of learning are:

1. Independent study
2. Peer-to-peer tutoring
3. One-on-one with teacher
4. Lecture
5. Team collaboration
6. Project-based learning
7. Distance learning
8. Learning with mobile technology
9. Student presentation
10. Internet-based research
11. Seminar-style instruction
12. Performance-based learning
13. Interdisciplinary study
14. Naturalist learning
15. Art-based learning
16. Social-emotional learning
17. Design-based learning
18. Storytelling
19. Team learning and teaching
20. Play and movement learning

Under the present paradigm of education, which is largely dictated by the way schools are designed, the library is there to do research and it is there to do independent study. The science lab is there to do hands-on work. The classroom is there for formal assimilation of content and some marginal skill building. The lunchroom is there primarily as a place to eat and, incidentally, to do some socializing, and on and on. In traditional school buildings, zoning the learning experience to different parts of the building makes it impossible for a teacher to design a curricular experience in which a student can go seamlessly from being in a lecture mode, to a collaborative mode, to a peer-tutoring mode, to a hands-on project mode, to a naturalist mode, and so on. In our design view, the physical school isn't zoned rigidly by activity. It is a place for holistic experiences, where multiple modalities of learning are accessible to both teachers and students on demand. In this design context, the learning experience may encompass a combination of seven learning modalities, or maybe eight of them, or even 12. The common space, for example, or the breakout space, or that mini-library we created, or that quiet zone, or the connections to the kitchen garden, are all there to form a rich palette, from which teachers and students can create multidisciplinary experiences. In this scenario, students experience multiple modalities of learning, which they can access based on the activity at hand and the needs of the task they are looking to accomplish. It is not necessary to schedule it, because if you schedule it, then the spontaneity is lost, and the creative flow that Csikszentmihalyi talks about is gone.[3] You have to be in flow in order to achieve anything, especially when engaging in creative practice. Architectural space has to reflect this new seamless and interdisciplinary world.

> We challenge schools to expose students to the interdisciplinary nature of everything they will encounter in their lives. It is hardly a secret that we are now in a changing world where almost every desirable job has interdisciplinary elements. This trend is not just here to stay but accelerating at a rate that makes it impossible to ignore.
>
> Real change from the old, familiar, but completely obsolete, educational model can only happen when we replace not just parts of the old model, but introduce a whole new one.[4]

NOTES

1 Prakash Nair, Roni Doctori, and Richard Elmore, *Learning by Design: Live, Play, Engage, Create* (Bangalore, India: Education Design Architects, 2019), 7.

2 Nair, Doctori, and Elmore, *Learning by Design*, 31.

3 See Mihaly Csikszentmihalyi, *Creativity: Flow and the Psychology of Discovery and Invention* (New York: Harper Collins, 1996).

4 Nair, Doctori, and Elmore, *Learning by Design*, 33–34.

COLLABORATING TO CREATE 9

Fred Leichter on the Collaborative Hive

EDITED BY ROBERT KELLY

Fred Leichter is the founding director of the Rick and Susan Sontag Center for Collaborative Creativity at the Claremont Colleges. Known as "the Hive," the center provides a place where students can form creative teams, be intellectually daring, and work collaboratively to address ambiguous challenges. It serves the five undergraduate Claremont Colleges: Pomona, Scripps, Claremont McKenna, Harvey Mudd, and Pitzer. Fred also serves as a clinical professor of engineering at Harvey Mudd and teaches human-centered design at the Hive.

Prior to these roles, Fred spent 25 years at Fidelity Investments in Boston, most recently as senior vice president of Design Thinking and Innovation. Fred designed Fidelity's first website in 1996 and created a thriving design discipline at the firm. Fred has also been a lecturer and fellow at the Stanford d.school, where he taught a range of classes such as Designing with Data, Designing for the Law, and Project Joy.

What is the Hive?

The Rick and Susan Sontag Center for Collaborative Creativity at the Claremont Colleges, known as "the Hive," sits at the intersection of five important, small liberal arts colleges in Southern California: Harvey Mudd College, which is a small science and engineering school of about 850 students; Claremont Mckenna, which is a liberal arts college focused generally on political science, government studies, policy, history, and humanities; Scripps College, which is an all-women's college; Pitzer College, which was founded in the late 1960s or early 1970s around themes of social justice; and Pomona College, which is the original college that was formed in the 1880s and is a kind of a classic elite liberal arts college. All five campuses are immediately adjacent to each other, and you can walk through the five campuses like one big campus. There's also a graduate program called Claremont Graduate University, which is attached. The Hive was put here to stimulate the creative confidence and creative capacity of students—give them a place where they can come to make things as part of the path toward understanding.

We think in terms of three levels of engagement. The first is an open invitation for students to walk into the place and start creating with supplies we have always on hand, such as big rolls of paper, sticky notes, sharpies, paint, sewing machines, some woodworking tools, a button maker. So, students are invited to come in and make things, no questions asked. All kinds of things get made: march posters, science walls, costumes for Halloween parties, creative projects just for self-satisfaction.

The second level of engagement involves a series of workshops that are not for credit and not mandatory. Sometimes these take the form of a pop-up class on introductory design thinking or empathetic listening, or an overview of product management, or workshops on blue-tape muraling or even on doodling. This creates an opportunity to get together with a group of people from varying backgrounds, stretch that creative muscle, and do things that the typical academic environment doesn't generally offer. Many students express a desire to get "unstuck" from their curriculum. We feel that the workshops open up avenues and, based on attendance, they are very successful. They involve creativity with a central collaborative dimension, working together across disciplines.

The third level of engagement is credit classes. I alternate teaching a class in human-centred design with two other faculty members. We have a huge waiting list to get into the class, with the selection criteria based more than anything on desire, and also diversity of experience, background, and perspective. The class works on big, ambiguous, real-world problems. Right now, it is redesigning the disaster preparation experience for another person, or the disaster recovery experience for another person or a marginalized group.

We have two overriding goals for the Hive. One is to enhance the creative confidence and creative capacity of students. The other is to help lead a renaissance of the liberal arts and liberal arts education, and to bring more making into a world of understanding.

Our Use of Space

In our space, everything is on wheels. We've created the "Hive space deck," which demonstrates 45 ways to set up your classroom. I started the space deck in our human-centred design class. We now have classes in subjects such as cell biology or gender studies or East Asian history using our space because they like the environment. We have offered some quick consultations to faculty, to help them modify their spaces and bring activities into their classes. We find that instructors and students want to literally shake up the space where teaching happens. We show them you can do this with intention. How can you set up your classroom with intention, to create a different atmosphere, a different environment that matches particular learning objectives? I taught a workshop for faculty on changing the physical set-up of classrooms. We talked about what you can do when it's easy to change the set-up—say, because everything's on wheels. We then took on the tougher challenge of how you change the learning environment of a space where the chairs are bolted to the floor, all facing in the same direction. What can you do there? We then talk about the five senses. What can you do to change the way it smells? What can you do to change the way it feels, or sounds, or looks? What are all the things that you can do with intention to change it? I've also been working with some clinical psychologists to look into research that shows people learn more or remember more when learning takes place in different environments. Take a list of Spanish vocabulary: if you try to learn it all sitting in a chair, you will learn less than if you move to different places—outside, inside—while learning the vocabulary. By learning in different places, you trigger different parts of your memory and you make different associations.

Research also shows that people go to their comfort zone at the family dinner table or in a classroom, that students quickly establish their territory for whatever reason. Students start to lock themselves into patterns based on where they are and the persona they assume—for example, whether they will be someone who raises their hand. They are inadvertently reducing their capacity to learn. When you come into my classroom, you can't go to your comfort zone, because it doesn't exist. I've moved it every single time.

The Hive is located in an old library building. It's quite informal, and its appearance is kind of messy. We have signs that grant permission to people. We have signs saying "yes, you can totally move things around," and "yes, you can totally hang out here," and "yes, you can have a club meeting here." It's a whole yes series, which is not what people expect. They usually are confronted by "no, you can't do this, you're in a role." We're trying to create that disposition of permission and a place where you can try things and experiment and play, and you can fail.

Developing Collaboration

I put together groups of students who are from different backgrounds and studying different subjects, because it is better for collaboration if people come at things from different perspectives. In this situation, ideas from different perspectives have equal weight. In collaborating, the team finds a way to best use the skills they bring together. At the end, the source and genesis of ideas that inform the product of the collaboration are not immediately clear to anybody, on the team or external to the team. Different people have touched the product along the way, and they are all sort of equally proud of it. Now, that does not always happen, but that's sort of my working definition of what good collaboration is. It's not just people showing up, being in a room together, or having a meeting. It's people making something together, and you can see the fingerprints of everybody on the product, and in the insight.

Here's an activity on collaborative creativity that I have adapted from a colleague at MIT and that I use in my class. I put groups of four or five together, and each group has an identical jigsaw puzzle on the table in front of them. I say: "Okay, first team to get the jigsaw puzzle done wins a box of Girl Scout cookies." I barely have the words out of my mouth before they're on it. They're saying, "You do the edges, you do the corners, you do this." They are tuned for that kind of competitive activity, where the outcome is known. So, then, just as the puzzles are starting to take shape, I tap one person from each team on the shoulder. They look up at me, thinking, "What are you doing?" I ask them to come with me to another room, to our main room, where there's a stack of fabric on the floor. I say: "Okay, new challenge. Make a quilt." They come back with all kinds of questions: "A quilt of what? How big? What shape?" I reply that it is up to them to decide. These students have now left the comfort of that jigsaw puzzle. Eventually, somebody gets on their knees as they sort of get an idea and they start doing it. I then go back to the jigsaw-puzzle room, and tap another person from each team on the shoulder, and they are looking at me as if to say, "Please, don't take me." I bring them out to the quilt room, and now they have to join this creative project that's underway. Some of them insinuate their way into the quilt project, and some just sort of stand there and watch. Some may break off and start doing something else, because there are no clear rules in the quilt room. At the end, I pull everybody into the quilt room, except I usually leave a team member from each group on the jigsaw puzzle, so somebody wins. In the quilt room, everybody's like, "Did we win?"

The debrief goes like this. I ask: "Which challenge were you more comfortable in?" They almost all admit they were more comfortable with the jigsaw puzzle, because they knew how to do that kind of thing and work together as a team on that. I then ask them to name another project or a problem in the real world that is like a jigsaw puzzle, where there's one right answer and there's a picture of it on the box. They sometimes suggest making furniture from IKEA, or making a cake from a mix, or working in an automobile factory.

Then, the question is: "Which of you want those jobs when you leave college?" Their response: "Oh, okay, you got us. I see where you're headed with this."

Next, I turn the conversation: "What happened in the room where you were working on the ambiguous problem, where you didn't have clear instructions? What happened when you joined a project underway, where it was a creative pursuit, or an ambiguous initiative, and you didn't know what was going on, or you didn't feel like you had input?" The point is: there is a lot to be learned to engage in those situations. I say that all of the projects in the class will look like the quilt, not the jigsaw puzzle. I will not know what the answer is. They will not know what the answer is. The goal is to try to figure out something that's worthwhile, and to find a way to work together, have fun, and make something new possible.

The class is about engaging in the design process in a collaborative setting. In many ways, the class involves a different way of doing than students are used to. In design, you have to learn to fail and realize that failure is part of the design process. Something has to go wrong. If your first idea—the one you come up with in week three, say—is the idea you come out with at the end, that's just a week-three idea with polish and shine. It's not going to satisfy this class, because it couldn't have been your best idea. Your best idea has to come from what you learned from things that didn't work, and that is often not your first idea. I guess that's my answer about the goal of collaborative creativity: not just that you're able to collaborate on some old-school fixed problem with a right answer, but you're able to collaborate where the answers are unknown.

Afterword

LONG LIVE THE PIONEERS, REBELS, AND MUTINEERS

The road to change and educational transformation is not an easy one. Many in education have grown to fear change of any kind. Yet change is inevitable. At what point does the white noise of not meeting the educational needs of educators and learners with obsolete structures and methods become so deafening as to cause action? Tolerating the white noise of dated perspectives also applies to broader global issues. At what point do we choose to act on depleted fish stocks around the planet, or on completely displaced populations because of the loss of arable land due to global warming? We have become anaesthetized and socialized into becoming passive consumers of virtually everything. Traditional educational discourses are very much the main reason for the perpetuation of this endemic disposition that has failed to equip educators and learners with the tools and disposition that empowers them to adapt to a changing world and, more importantly, to create positive change. At what point do we choose to act on creating a new educational way of being in the world that is not accountable to standardized, consumption-intense sensibilities that have become increasingly irrelevant and largely obsolete? How is this perpetual chain broken?

The title of this afterword, "Long Live the Pioneers, Rebels and Mutineers," and the headings in the content that follows are lyrics from the song "Renegades" by the X Ambassadors (2015). These words speak to a disposition that we have to instill in all educators and learners, to embody the experimentation, research, new practices, and new ways of being in education for the way forward, where everything is questioned and where we don't succumb to Koestler's "anaesthesia of conditioning."

The concept of Clay Christensen's (2016) disruptive innovation, or the concepts of creative destruction (Diamond, 2019) or self-disruptive innovation, come into play here for educational organizations too impervious to fundamental change to transform from within. Carey (2015) speaks about the need for large liberal arts institutions to adapt as their business models become obsolete with the emergence of the "university of everywhere" concept. People want to learn and to be empowered to create their own futures. Learning from experts in the field is easily accessible from anywhere on the planet, and it has become very easy for anyone to create their own relevant educational journeys. Two years ago, while attending an education conference, I was listening to a panel of indigenous K to 12 educators talk about their experiences in grade school. One of them, talking about his high school experience, said, "I didn't want to go to school, I just wanted to learn." I thought it was quite profound that he didn't associate school with learning. Fundamental change about our perceptions and practice of what education is will only occur with substantial reframing that starts with recognizing all of the factors that inform the profound inertia that precludes change.

Educational transformation begins on so many fronts. It begins in teacher education that equips educators with high creative and collaborative capacities through firsthand experience, so that they will be able to create innovative educational environments for learners and new ways of being in education. We need to be developing educators who will lead transformation through creativity and collaboration. It begins with many in the ivory tower of academia becoming relevant and accountable to educators and learners on the shop floor, and not just to others in the tower. It begins with adapting a disposition of design where obstacles are not roadblocks, but mere constraints on the road to developing something new and wondrous for educators and learners. Failure in this context is a normal part of prototyping on the path to innovation, not a punitive symbol from an obsolete system.

Go Forth and Have No Fear

It begins with administrators and government officials having the courage and foresight to create adhocratic educational spaces of experimentation and invention, as a form of disruptive innovation, to lead the way forward. It begins by engaging in deep and active empathetic listening with learners and with each other.

Come Close and Lend an Ear

It begins with a new ecosystem of neolearning in education that focuses on collaborative creativity at the centre of a transformative ecosystem that empowers all involved. The mobilization of this potential has such incredible promise for everyone and everything. It is an invitation, right there in front of all of us, to move away from an obsolete, disproportionate focus on passive consumption of knowledge as mainstream educational practice. It is an invitation to equip and empower educators and learners through collaborative creativity and innovation to act for the benefit of all. How could anyone refuse this offer?

Key Terms for Creative Development and Collaborative Creativity in Educational Practice

This list compiles terms from this book and from its companion volume, *Creative Development: Transforming Education through Design Thinking, Innovation, and Invention* (Kelly, 2016). These terms describe ideas and vocabulary at the core of the work of educators striving to establish educational cultures conducive to creative development and collaborative creativity.

adhocracy: a flattened, amorphous organizational structure designed to enable fluid innovation and creative practice characterized by the free movement of expert resources as needed

assets to access: the transformative dynamic where educational focus shifts from hoarding and accumulating knowledge to accessing knowledge

assessment anxiety: the fear of appearing less competent in front of peers because of overt comparison due to assessment

assessment as learning: a process of developing and supporting metacognition for students focusing on the role of the student as the critical connector between assessment and learning; involves students monitoring their own learning and using the feedback from this monitoring to make adjustments, adaptations, and even major changes in what they understand

assessment by metaphor: an example of formative assessment to encourage dialogic assessment, whereby a metaphor is applied to a learning outcome to stimulate discussion and feedback on student initiatives

assessment for learning: typically formative in nature; designed to give teachers information to modify and differentiate teaching and learning activities, acknowledging that individual students learn in idiosyncratic ways

assessment of learning: summative in nature; used to confirm what students know and can do, to demonstrate whether they have achieved curriculum outcomes and, occasionally, to show how they are ranked in relation to others

atelier: an interdisciplinary studio space introduced into the Reggio Emilia preschools by Loris Malaguzzi

big-C creativity: creativity that has considerable impact in a field or discipline

brainstorming: the production of ideas or problem resolutions through group conversation and interaction

collaboration: highly interactive group of two or more people engaged in an initiative where group members bring complementary skill sets to each other to create to potential that was not necessarily attainable by an individual working alone or alongside other individuals

collaborative/communicative development: a cofoundational creative developmental strand focused on the collaboration and communication skills essential for the practice of collaborative creativity; it amplifies and enhances the potential of the other interrelated creative development strands

collaborative creativity: a group of two or more individuals with a shared purpose and complementary skills engaged in a sequence of thoughts and actions that leads to novel adaptive production that would be impossible or highly unlikely to achieve as individuals

connectivity: the capacity for interconnection between systems, processes, or concepts

consume to create: the transformative dynamic that shifts the focus of education from equipping learners with content knowledge to instilling in learners an innate dispositional capacity for collaborative creativity, which enables application of discipline knowledge and processes for innovation

convergent thinking: the process of narrowing down a list of alternatives to select those with the greatest potential for problem resolution through comparative analysis

cooperation: a group of two or more people working on task completion that may or may not involve interactivity among those involved

cooperative/reflective assessment: a type of co-reflective formative assessment, characterized by writing-intense dialogic assessment, in which key developmental and process questions are developed between the student and educator specific to a creative exploration and are answered by both as points of discussion

creative confidence: the positive feeling derived from validation received through taking risks and recognizing that all ideas that one creates have value; a term associated with design thinking practice at Stanford's d.school

creative development: the growth of one's creative capacity from adaptive/intuitive creativity to encompass the ability to engage in increasingly complex sustained creative practice

creative sustain development: the capacity to engage in recurrent iterations of idea generation and prototype experimentation of increasing complexity over extended periods of time (in this context, *sustain* comes from music, where it means prolonging the resonance of a note or chord); one of several interrelated creative development strands

creativity: the sequence of thoughts and actions that leads to a novel, adaptive production (Lubart, 2000)

critical thinking: the ability to explore a problem, question, or situation; integrate all the available information about it; arrive at a solution or hypothesis; and justify one's position (Warnick & Inch, 1994)

critical thinking development: one of eight interrelated creative development strands involving the application of critical-thinking skills to compare and assess potential solutions to a problem

deep listening: the process of engaging in the stages of attentive, interpretive, empathetic, and generative listening

design process: the methods and processes for investigating problems, acquiring information, analyzing knowledge, developing alternatives, and prototyping in the design and planning fields across a wide range of disciplines; also called contextual creative problem-solving; defined by IDEO (2012) as the stages of discovery, interpretation, ideation, experimentation, and evolution

diagnostic assessment: a type of assessment often used in the context of detecting basic skill deficits and learner strengths to inform remediation and differentiated instructional strategies

dialogic assessment: a form of assessment based on dialogue between student and educator, where the educator acts as mentor or coach, that is focused on the development of student work

didactic to dialogic: the transformative dynamic where educational practice shifts from traditional lecture practices to highly interactive practice focused on collaborative creativity

discipline-complexity development: a creative development strand involving the growth in understanding of the content, processes, and complexities of a discipline

disposition: the tendency to act in a certain manner under given circumstances, which increases the likelihood that effective actions will be taken when confronted with problematic situations (Costa & Kallick, 2014)

dissociation: an emotional detachment from the learning environment

divergent-convergent pulse: in idea generation, a series of repeated divergent/convergent phases in which numerous ideas are generated and then a small number are chosen as promising solutions

divergent thinking: the expansive development of alternative resolutions through idea generation and prototype experimentation

early closure: the tendency to close the idea generation process early; usually the result of conditioning developed when most learning experience outcomes are known

ecosystem: the complex of living organisms, their physical environment, and all their interrelationships in a particular unit of space

elaboration: the ability to add complexities to existing forms

enterprise: a disposition or initiative that reflects the tackling of difficult or complex problems in new ways

entrepreneurship: the pursuit of opportunity beyond resources controlled; involving a mindset to imagine new ways to solve problems and create value (Eisenmann, 2013)

experimentational development: growth of the capacity to consistently test ideas as potential solutions to set problems, through prototyping in the medium of the field or discipline where the creative production occurs; one of several interrelated creative development strands

extrinsic motivation: motivation for task engagement and task completion that is external to the student

feedback spiral: a recursive, cyclical process designed for learners and educators to constantly gather data that is analyzed and interpreted for self-learning and self-modifying actions

flexibility: the ability to abandon old ways and adapt to a new way of thinking

fluency: the capacity to effortlessly generate ideas and alternatives in creative practice

formative assessment: a range of formal and informal assessment procedures that typically involves qualitative feedback (rather than scores) to enhance student development in process engagement and performance

fourth sector business: a business approach that integrates social and environmental aims, often embodying features like fair compensation, environmental responsibility, community service, and contribution of profits to the common good

gifting economy: the practice among some Indigenous Peoples of gaining status by giving gifts to others, where nothing is owned

historiometrics: a quantitative method of statistical analysis of an individual's accomplishments that places the individual's creative practice on a vertical scale of importance relative to the fields where the practice occurred

hypercompetitiveness: a cultural phenomenon in which there is an overemphasis on being at the top of vertical comparison hierarchies

hyperconsumption: a cultural phenomenon in which a disproportionate focus is placed on the accumulation of commodities, information, wealth, and so on

idea mapping: a graphical method of tracking the intersection of ideas with other stimuli to observe the development of new idea combinations and the creation of new ideas

ideation: a purposeful stage in the creative process for the generation of ideas and alternatives

ideation development: the growth and development of the capacity to generate ideas

ideation waves: the compounding of an idea as it goes through successive hybridizations by combining with new ideas and continually creating new iterations

illumination: a time of convergence when thoughts come together for potential solutions

imagination: a special feature or form of human thought characterized by the ability of an individual to reproduce images or concepts originally derived from basic senses but now reflected in one's consciousness as memories, fantasies, and future plans

incubation: an active subconscious stage where ideas are reorganized and elaborated upon

innovation: an application of creative design practice in which an idea is introduced and applied to a situation that benefits the job, process, or organization, or the development of a product where this occurs

innovative creativity: a form of sustained creative practice involving the redesign or modification of an existing form, product, or system; usually associated with business and industry

interdisciplinary: creative practice across more than one discipline

interpretive creativity: a form of sustained creative practice involving the redesign, modification, evolution, or interpretation of existing work or forms often associated with the arts

intrinsic motivation: the drive to engage in a learning experience or creative exploration that comes from within an individual through substantial personal interest

intuitive/adaptive creativity: the creative acts that are part of everyday living

invention: the application of creativity that leads to the development of something new across any number of fields or disciplines

inventive creativity: a form of sustained creative practice involving the creation of original work across disciplines

inventive momentum: a strong, creative dynamic that develops in high-stimulus, highly generative, and experimentational environments

inventive structure: the defined parameters of a creative exploration that emerges after considerable idea generation and experimentation

learning creatively: the development of novel responses or solutions to curriculum-content problems or dilemmas largely through creative problem-solving

learning to create: the creation of personally meaningful original work through sustained creative practice that goes well beyond the demands of traditional curriculum content

little-c creativity: the creativity that every human being engages in on a daily basis

machine bureaucracy: a management structure with a high degree of formalization and specialization in which decisions are largely made at the top level and organization output is largely focused on standardization

makerspace: an interdisciplinary studio space that is a collaborative work area for tinkering, design, and invention

measurement to development: the transformative dynamic where educational assessment shifts from summative, quantitative assessment practice to metacognitive, dialogic assessment practice, which embodies mentoring and collaborative relationship between the educator and learner, with heightened focus on collaborative and creative development

metacognition: thinking about and understanding one's own cognitive processes

metaphorical thinking: a mental process in which comparisons are made between qualities of objects that are usually considered in separate classifications, enabling new constructs to be formed and comfort with ambiguity

mindshift: a move from designing for ego-centric purposes to broader human-centred goals

moai: the Okinawan concept of a group of friends that are together for life, and that collaborate and care for each other's needs

originality: a creative response that is novel, remote, and statistically unusual, or a departure from previous responses relative to an individual's previous creative output or relative to a field or discipline

outcomes known: a learning experience characterized by the restating and retelling of known responses

outcomes unknown: a learning experience characterized by explorations that are set in motion without exact knowledge of the form of the final outcome

passion: an intense emotional connection to engaged creative production

passive to interactive: the transformative dynamic that shifts education from passive, consumption-intense practice to a highly interactive educational practice of collaborative creativity

pedagogy: the leadership of children; often describing diverse approaches to teaching

personal/historical creativity: a sequence of thoughts and actions that leads to novel, adaptive production compared to the previous production of the individual or group

plussing: in collaborative idea generation, the act of accepting any idea and adding to it

preinventive structure: the loosely defined parameters for a creative exploration within a field or discipline that are wide enough to enable further play and exploration, but defined enough to prevent floundering from lack of focus

preparation: the notion of initial problem setting, or dealing with a discordance, that requires some sort of resolution for which the outcome is unknown

principle of infinite potentials: the belief that any idea has the potential for an infinite number of combinations and recombinations with other ideas, and a corresponding belief that, as the creator of ideas, anyone has infinite potentials specific to ideation and ultimately to creative production

principle of interrelatedness: a foundational belief that every organic and inorganic entity is connected, requiring a heightened state of empathy to enable collaborative, creative problem-solving

principle of perpetual change: a foundational understanding that education should enable participants to adapt to perpetual change and to create positive perpetual change

prototyping: a preliminary design form to test problem-resolution concepts to enable design refinement in the materials or currency of the discipline where the design is occurring

push to pull: the transformative dynamic that shifts educational practice from imposed mandated curricula to curricula built around learner needs and interests

redefinition: the capacity to give up traditional interpretations and invent new ones

reframing: the questioning and analysis of traditional beliefs about education and ways of doing from the perspective of the relevance of those beliefs for adapting to rapid change and creating positive change

research/investigative development: growth in the capacity to bring discipline knowledge and stimuli to sustained creative practice through a disposition that is relentless in collecting data from any source; one of eight interrelated creative development strands

resocialization: learning complete new ways of doing by creating and functioning in an immersive culture that embodies that new way of doing

self-instigative development: growth in the capacity to engage in an intrinsically motivated, creative exploration that is intellectually and emotionally meaningful and relevant; one of eight interrelated creative development strands

skew effects: ingrained behavioural patterns or organizational predispositions that undermine transformative initiatives

sociocultural creativity: the sequence of thoughts and actions by which an individual or group produces a perceptible product that is both novel and useful, as defined within the social context of an established field or domain and its members

sociogogy: an educational discourse where teachers and students are learning "companions" leading one another, entailing a whole new framework for learning and co-creating knowledge

statusless environment: a learning environment that suppresses vertical hierarchies for the purpose of providing a safe, collaborative space for participants to be vulnerable in the sharing of ideas while precluding harsh judgement

STEM: an acronym for the disciplines of science, technology, engineering, and mathematics, often used in the context of improving science and technology development in education; STEM becomes STEAM when A for art and design is added to the acronym

summative assessment: a form of assessment that demonstrates the extent of a learner's success in meeting the assessment criteria used to gauge the intended learning outcomes of a module or program, and which contributes to a quantifiable final grade

sustained creativity: the capacity to engage in successive iterations of idea generation and experimentation in creative practice over time

tinkering: exploratory and experimental repair, making, and inventing in a wide range of media

tolerance of ambiguity: the willingness to accept some uncertainty, precluding rigidity in thinking

unschooling: a purely democratic form of schooling in which learning decisions lie almost completely with the student

verification: the point in the creative process at which thoughts are given form to test whether they actually work as solutions

References

Allison, M. (2015, June 4). Complexity in systems, organizations and the workplace. *WorkDesign Magazine*. Retrieved from https://workdesign.com/2015/06/complexity-in-systems-organizations-and-the-workplace/

Altidor, W. (2017). *Creative courage*. Hoboken, NJ: John Wiley and Sons.

Amabile, T., & Pratt, M. (2016). The dynamic componential model of creativity and innovation in organizations: Making progress, making meaning. *Research in Organizational Behavior, 37*, 157–183.

Benammar, K. (2012). *Reframing: The art of thinking differently*. Amsterdam: Boom.

Benammar, K., van Dijk, M., & Wolfe, R. (2014, April 16). The golden opportunity of paradigm shifts. THNK website. Retrieved from https://www.thnk.org/insights/the-golden-opportunity-of-paradigm-shifts/

Carey, K. (2015). *The end of college*. New York: Riverbend Books.

Cheek, D. W. (2015). A panoramic view of the future of learning and the role of design(ers). In B. Hokanson, G. Clinto, & M. W. Tracey (Eds.), *The design of learning experience: Creating the future of educational technology* (5–37). Dordrecht: Springer.

Christensen, C. (2016). *The innovator's dilemma: When new technologies cause great firms to fail.* (3rd ed.). Boston: Harvard Business Review Press.

Cohen, G. (2014, December 10). Mastering the 4 levels of listening. *The Business Journals.* Retrieved from https://www.bizjournals.com/bizjournals/how-to/growth-strategies/2014/12/mastering-the-4-levels-of-listening.html

Costa, A. L., & Kallick, B. (2014). *Dispositions: Reframing teaching and learning.* Thousand Oaks: Corwin Press.

Csikszentmihalyi, M. (1996). *Creativity: Flow and the psychology of discovery and invention*. New York: Harper Collins.

Diamond, A. (2019). *Openness to creative destruction*. New York: Oxford University Press.

Doorley, S., & Witthoft, S. (2012). *Make space: How to set the stage for creative collaboration*. Hoboken, NJ: John Wiley & Sons.

Eisenmann, T. R. (2013, January 10). Entrepreneurship: A working definition. *Harvard Business Review*. Retrieved from https://hbr.org/2013/01/what-is-entrepreneurship

Fischer, C., Malycha, C., & Schafmann, E. (2019). The influence of intrinsic motivation and synergistic extrinsic factors on creativity and innovation. *Frontiers in Psychology, 10*, 137. doi: 10.3389/fpsyg.2019.00137

Gardner, H. (1980). *Artful scribbles: The significance of children's drawings*. New York: Basic Books.

Gardner, H. (2016). *Smart collaboration*. Boston: Harvard Business Review Press.

Gloor, P. (2017). *Swarm leadership and the collective mind*. Bingley, UK: Emerald Publishing.

Gotz, I. (1981). On defining creativity. *Journal of Aesthetics and Art Criticism, 39*, 297–301.

Guilford, J. (1959). Traits of creativity. In H. Anderson (Ed.), *Creativity and its cultivation* (pp. 142–161). New York: Harper.

Hagel, J., & Brown, J. (2005). From push to pull: Emerging models for mobilizing resources. Working paper. Retrieved from http://www.johnhagel.com/paper_pushpull.pdf

Hagel, J., Brown, J., & Davison, L. (2010). *The power of pull: How small moves, smartly made, can set big things in motion*. New York: Deloitte Development LLC.

IDEO (2012). Design thinking toolkit for educators (2nd ed.). Retrieved from https://designthinkingforeducators.com/toolkit/

Kaufmann, J. C., Plucker, J. A., & Baer, J. (2008). *Essentials of creativity assessment*. Hoboken, NJ: Wiley & Sons.

Kelly, R. (2012). *Educating for creativity: A global conversation*. Edmonton, Canada: Brush Education.

Kelly, R. (2016). *Creative development: Transforming education through design thinking, innovation, and invention*. Edmonton, Canada: Brush Education.

Kelly, R., & Leggo, C. (Eds.). (2008). *Creative expression, creative education: Creativity as a primary rationale for education*. Calgary, Canada: Detselig.

KnowledgeWorks Forecast 5.0: The Future of Learning: Navigating the Future of Learning. (2018). Retrieved from https://knowledgeworks.org/resources/forecast-5/

Koestler, A. (1964). *The act of creation*. London, UK: Hutchinson.

Lehrer, J. (2012). *Imagine: How creativity works*. Boston: Houghton Mifflin Harcourt.

Leonard, A. (2018). Moai: This tradition is why Okinawan people live longer, better. Blue Zones website. Retrieved from https://www.bluezones.com/2018/08/moai-this-tradition-is-why-okinawan-people-live-longer-better/

Leonard, K., & Yorton, T. (2015). *Yes, and*. New York: Harper Collins.

Lubart, T. I. (2000). Models of creative process: Past, present and future. *Creativity Research Journal, 13*, 295–308.

Mintzberg, H. (1989). *Mintzberg on management*. New York: The Free Press.

Nair, P. (2014). *Blueprint for tomorrow: Redesigning schools for student-centered learning*. Cambridge, MA: Harvard Education Press.

Nair, P., & Doctori, R. (2019). *Learning by design*. Tampa: Education Design Architects.

Nelson, R. (2008, September 8). Learning and working in the collaborative age. Edutopia website. Retrieved from https://www.edutopia.org/randy-nelson-school-to-career-video

Ontario Ministry of Education. (2013). *Learning for all: A guide to effective assessment and instruction for all students.* Toronto: Government of Ontario.

Organisation for Economic Co-operation and Development (2018). The future of education and skills: Education 2030. Retrieved from https://www.oecd.org/education/2030/E2030%20Position%20Paper%20(05.04.2018).pdf

Osborn, A. (1963). *Applied imagination.* New York: Scribner.

Page, S. (2007). *The difference.* Princeton: Princeton University Press.

Piirto, J. (2004). *Understanding creativity.* Scottsdale, AZ: Great Potential Press.

Plucker, J., Beghetto, R., & Dow, G. (2004). Why isn't creativity more important to educational psychologists? Potentials, pitfalls, and future directions in creativity research. *Educational Psychologist, 39*, 83–96.

Prince, K., Saveri, A., & Swanson, J. (2015, August 19). Exploring the future education workforce: New roles for an expanding learning ecosystem. KnowledgeWorks website. Retrieved from https://knowledgeworks.org/resources/future-education-workforce-roles-ecosystem/

Runco, M. (2014). *Creativity: Theories and themes: Research, development and practice* (2nd ed.). San Diego, CA: Academic Press.

Saveri, A., & Chwierut, M. (2011, August 9). The future of learning agents and disruptive innovation. KnowledgeWorks website. Retrieved from https://knowledgeworks.org/resources/future-learning-agents-disruption/

Sawyer, K. (2012). *Explaining creativity: The science of innovation.* New York: Oxford University Press.

Sawyer, K. (2017). *Group genius: The creative power of collaboration* (Rev. ed.). New York: Basic Books.

Scharmer, O. (2018). *The essentials of theory U: Core principles and applications.* Oakland, CA: Berrett-Koehler Publishers.

Scharmer, O., & Kaufer, K. (2013). *Leading from the emerging future: From ego-system to eco-system economies.* Oakland, CA: Berrett-Koehler Publishers.

Schrage, M. (1990). *Shared minds: The new technologies of collaboration.* New York: Random House.

Schrage, M. (2015, March 23). Collaboration, from the Wright brothers to robots. *Harvard Business Review.* Retrieved from https://hbr.org/2015/03/collaboration-from-the-wright-brothers-to-robots

Simonton, D. (2016). Defining creativity: Don't we also need to define what is not creative? *Journal of Creative Behavior, 52* (1), 80–90.

Smith, G. (1998). Idea generation techniques: A formulary of active ingredients. *Journal of Creative Behavior, 32* (2), 107–133.

Spitzer, T. (2018). *The power of collaboration.* Wayne, NJ: Career Press.

Starko, A. J. (2010). *Creativity in the classroom* (4th ed.). New York: Routledge.

Tharp, B. (2009). Four organizational culture types. Retrieved from https://pdfs.semanticscholar.org/b0e2/fd342fcf402920e264f15070276b79be1e25.pdf

ThoughtFarmer. (2018, March 15). What collaboration really means [Blog post]. Retrieved from https://www.thoughtfarmer.com/blog/what-collaboration-really-means/

United Nations. (2019). Sustainable development goals. Retrieved from https://www.un.org/sustainabledevelopment/

Waks, L. J. (2014). *Education 2.0: The learning web revolution and the transformation of the school.* Boulder, CO: Paradigm Books.

Wallas, G. (1926). *The art of thought.* New York: Harcourt Brace.

Warnick, B., & Inch, E. (1994). *Critical thinking and communicatio*n (2nd ed.). New York: MacMillan.

Western and Northern Protocol for Collaboration in Education (2006). *Rethinking classroom assessment with purpose in mind.* Retrieved from https://digitalcollection.gov.mb.ca/awweb/pdfopener?smd=1&did=12503&md=1

X Ambassadors (2015). Renegades. Retrieved from https://genius.com/X-ambassadors-renegades-lyrics

Index

About the Author

Educator, author, artist, and keynote speaker Robert Kelly is a recognized leader in the fields of collaborative creativity, creative development, design thinking for innovation, and transformational educational practice. He is academic coordinator of the Collaborative Creativity & Design Thinking for Innovation graduate program in the Werklund School of Education, and an associate professor at the University of Calgary. Robert has been an invited visiting scholar at several postsecondary institutions for his work in the field of collaborative creativity. As a changemaker, he is a fervent advocate of educational transformation to adapt to rapid sociocultural, economic, and technological change, and to empower all to create positive change for the benefit of others.

His previous titles in the field of creativity in education include *Creative Development: Transforming Education through Design Thinking, Innovation, and Invention* (2016), *Educating for Creativity: A Global Conversation* (2012), and *Creative Expression, Creative Education: Creativity as a Primary Rationale for Education* (2012) (coedited with Carl Leggo).

Robert is profiled on the University of Calgary's Great Teachers website, and has been a featured national and international keynote speaker on the topics of collaborative creativity, educational transformation, and creative development in education.

Contact: rkelly@ucalgary.ca Website: www.robertkelly.ca